UPW

Tony Robbins

4/9/14

Pass -

Trello·com   CS

Inabit 1

Love

Media

C

Select all layers

Cmd+E

Flaten Image

ISBN: 1494219840
ISBN-13: 978-1494219840

Dedicated to my four sons
Niels, Victor, Oliver and Tim.

Niels for introducing me to Social Media when he blogged
during his travels in South East Asia, many years ago.

Victor for showing me that true relationships happen in real
life and not only online.

Oliver for showing that focus on what you want will give
you the outcome you desire.

And Tim for keeping me up to date on the latest trends in
Social Media.

MARC CAMPMAN

"Some people see things as they are and say why. I dream things that never were and say why not?"

George Bernard Shaw

MARC CAMPMAN

CONTENTS

MARC CAMPMAN

ACKNOWLEDGMENTS

Thank you to my wife Noor who inspired me to write this book and who taught me the art of writing. I'm most grateful to you.

And thanks to Mark Young, my business partner in Love Social Media, who gave me the opportunity to develop and promote my Social Media skills on a scale that would not have been possible without him.

And most of all, thanks to the hundreds of people who attended my workshops and strategy sessions. And to those who will do so in the future.

You make me wake up every morning with the desire to continue living my dream.

MARC CAMPMAN

FOREWORD

Let me take you back to June 1995, 1st Street, San Jose California, the heart of Silicon Valley. We have 20 customers from Europe visiting our PC manufacturing site. They are sitting in awe in our high tech PC demonstration centre getting a demo on the latest and greatest in PC technology. Multimedia PCs and Desktop video conferencing. Breakthrough technology, never seen before. But none of them are prepared for what I am about to show them. I step on the stage and I start my presentation with a simple question. "Who of you has ever surfed the Web?" 20 pairs of eyes looked at me in bewilderment. They didn't have a clue. One person answered: "We're in California. So don't you surf the waves?" Obviously, nobody had ever heard of the World Wide Web. So I start my presentation with the words "Well, let me take you on a journey. Let's surf the web". Only years later I realised I was probably one of the first who surfed the Internet.

Fast-forward 6 years. January 2001. Rotterdam Netherlands. Graduation day for 20 students of the International Masters Degree in Corporate Communications at the Erasmus University in Rotterdam. I am one them. My thesis is titled "Branding.com. How to build brand leadership in the new economy". Over the years I got so excited about the dot.com bubble that I dedicated my thesis to this subject. I did a study how brands like Google, Yahoo, eBay and Amazon.com managed to build a global brand in a fraction of the time that it took companies like IBM, Coca Cola or Cisco to build theirs. The professor announces the winner of the Shell Stimulation Award of Excellence in Corporate Communication. "And the winner is: Branding.com. How to build brand leadership in the new economy".

Fast-forward 12 years. June 2013. Kings Langley, England. I am clearing the attic. In a dark corner I find a box with documents, reports and articles that I collected during my early career. In this box I also find a printed copy of my thesis "Branding.com. How to build brand leadership in the new economy". I drop everything and I start reading what I wrote 12 years ago. And then my eye falls on one of the research propositions:

"Proposition 5: The strength of the dot.com brand is (positively) related to the quality of the (personalised) content delivery and interaction on their web site."

I was astonished. Isn't this what Social Media is all about? Content and Interaction? How could I have been able to predict Social Media, as far back as the year 2001? Is that why I won the award? Is that why I got so excited about the subject of Social Media? Was this a sign on the wall that I would become an expert in this field?

Or was there something else that made me state this in 2001, many years before businesses really saw the potential of Social Media? I think there was. It is called common sense. It is all about the basics of people communicating with people. When people communicate with each other they interact as people and talk about the things that are relevant to them. They do not communicate as robots. The web 2.0, or the interactive web, has taken this type of communication to the business world. If a brand wants to connect with its customers they have to make themselves relevant. They can only do that if they listen to the customer to find out what is important to them.

This is why I love Social Media. It puts the customer in the driving seat. It forces companies to be transparent, to be available everywhere and to connect with customers instead of selling to them. It is a new kind of relationship.

By founding "Love Social Media" we (my business partner Mark Young and myself) created a way to share our love for Social Media with people and businesses. We challenge the relationships that companies have with their customers. We do this by offering Social Media training and services that are getting to the heart of customer conversations and relationships. This book will hopefully inspire you to love your customers just a little bit more.

Marc Campman
Social Media Playmaker
London, England
January 2014

MARC CAMPMAN

INTRODUCTION

The funny thing about Social Media is that everybody in some way is already using it, but not where you expect. Not on Facebook or on Twitter, but in real life. In real life people make friends, have conversations, talk about good and bad experiences, listen to music, go to concerts, watch TV and go to the cinema to watch movies. It can't get more social than this and it all happens in the real world. Social Media is nothing more than taking these offline experiences into the online world. And for people and businesses this opens a new world of connections. A world that goes beyond borders, rules or regulations.

There's no better way to explain this than using the analogy of dating. When you date, you first go to places where you meet people. You go to parties, bars, nightclubs or any other place where you can meet people. When you meet someone that seems nice, you get into a conversation. You break the ice. You start to build your reputation. If the other person likes you and likes what you say, he or she might be interested in meeting you again. Maybe you become friends or even lovers. You may get married and stay together for the rest of your life. Or, when you don't invest in maintaining your relationship you could end up with a divorce.

In business it works exactly the same way. Instead, parties become exhibitions, bars become networking events and the movie in the cinema becomes your marketing campaign. But the objectives are the same. You are trying to find new customers. You start talking to prospects and if they like what they hear, they will marry you, or in business terms, they will buy from you. If you do the right things, they will buy from you again and maybe introduce you to some of their friends. But if you mess up, they will divorce you. They will drop you as a supplier and go to your competition.

Following this analogy you could say that for businesses Social Media is like online dating. You are trying to connect with people online (prospects, customers, influencers). You are going to give them content they like in order to grow your online reputation. When they convert this reputation into trust, they are happy to engage in a relationship with you. In other words, they are happy to become your customer. If you put enough effort in your Social Media, they will buy from you again and they will recommend you to their friends.

No-one understands this concept better than us at Love Social Media. Because we love Social Media. We love it so much that we even invented a term for this. FLIRT. Social Media is all about flirting with the customer. FLIRT is our acronym for 5 simple steps to socialise your business. 5 steps to implement Social Media to successfully grow your business.

In this book you will learn how to flirt. How to apply each step to your business.

Here's a quick rundown of what FLIRT stands for:

F is for Focus. This is the starting point of your Social Media. Some of the questions you will need to answer when you start your Social Media are; Why are you using Social Media? What are your objectives? Who are you targeting? What is your positioning? What are the keywords of your business? The secret is to focus. The better you focus on your niche, the more unique and inspiring you are, the more successful you will be with your Social Media.

L is for Listen. Online listening is a vital component of your Social Media. Some people use Social Media just to listen. Other people listen online to make sure the content they share resonates with their followers. When you listen, you listen to where your clients hang out. What social networks they use and what they talk about. You listen to your key influencers, your favourite bloggers. You listen to trends in the market place and you listen to your customers and your competitors. Instead of you having to go to all these websites, you let them come to your online listening station.

I is for Integration. If you know where your clients hang out, obviously, you want to be there as well. So you are going to set up your own social networks. Facebook, Twitter, LinkedIn, Google+, Youtube, Pinterest or Instagram. Each has its own characteristics. But the common elements are your profile, your branding and your key messages. It is vital that they are consistent. In this stage you are also going to integrate your social networks and start creating content through blogging, video or podcasting.

R is for Reaching Out. This is a vital part of your Social Media. Being on Social Media networks isn't enough. You need to drive people to your Social Media sites by sharing good content. The better your content, the quicker you will build your reputation and the more people will connect with you and go to your web site to find out more about you. Running campaigns is a vital part of this. Through innovative Social Media campaigns you can really accelerate this process of growing your communities.

T is for Track. You can't change what you cannot measure. Questions you need to ask yourself include; Are you achieving your objectives? Are you growing your communities? What content works and what doesn't? How much traffic are you getting to your sites? How much engagement is there on your sites? What is the sentiment of comments? You can learn a lot when you analyse all this and you can use this knowledge to alter your strategy if required. As such, your Tracking feeds your Focus and the FLIRT process becomes a continuous circle.

This is why we love Social Media and why we love to challenge the relationships that companies have with their customers. Because we passionately believe that Social Media will get you to the heart and soul of the relationships and conversations you have with your customers.

THE BIGGER PICTURE

Over one hour of video is being uploaded on Youtube every second which is a phenomenal amount. Can you imagine the legacy of content that we are creating for future generations? The fact that Facebook has over a billion subscribers is not really significant. What is important is that over one billion items are "Liked" on Facebook every day. This shows that people are engaging on it. People are using Facebook not just to look at it but to share, like and comment. 350 million photos are being uploaded on Facebook every day.

Here's a snap shot of some amazing social media statistics and facts of 2013:

- 23% of Facebook users check their account over 5 times a day.
- Twitter's fastest growing demographic is 55-64 year olds
- 60% of Twitter users access it from their mobile
- There are over 343 million active users on Google+
- The +1 button is served 5 billion times per day

- 67% of Google+ users are male
- There are over 3 million Linkedin company pages
- More than 16 billion photos have been uploaded to Instagram
- Food is the top category discussed on Pinterest at 57%
- There are over 1 billion unique monthly visitors on YouTube

(Source: mediabistro.com, facebook.com, expandedramblings.com, socialmediaexaminer.com)

Social Media is everywhere; we can no longer avoid it. People are using Social Media and more and more businesses start to understand that they have to get onto it as well. Otherwise, they miss an opportunity.

What is Social Media?

Let's start with the basics. What does Social Media mean? If we would ask for a definition, how would you define Social Media? When I explain Social Media in my workshops, I use my three "Cs" of Social Media. Social Media is all about Content, Communities and Campaigns. The better your content, the easier it is to build communities. And you can push that process by launching campaigns to promote your content. That's the whole essence of Social Media. It is not about Facebook. It is not about Twitter. They may have lost their dominance next year. But it is about what really matters - Content. Within this context, Social Media can be defined as:

"Online tools that people use to share content, profiles, opinions, insights, experiences, perspectives and media itself, thus facilitating conversations and interaction online between groups of people. These tools include blogs, message boards, podcasts, micro blogs, bookmarks, networks, communities, wikis, and vlogs." (WebProNews.com)

Another definition takes it from another perspective.

"A new set of internet tools that enable shared community experiences, both online and in person." (Technology in Translation)

I like the "in person" aspect of this definition because at the end, it happens in the offline world. If people want to buy a product, they still buy it from a person and that happens in the offline world. So mixing both online and offline is key in Social Media.

It is all driven by the way we consume media these days. 10 years ago, we primarily consumed media through TV, Radio, magazines, billboards or direct mail. Then the first online portals came out like Yahoo and they offered an additional channel of communication. Nowadays, most of our media exposure happens online. Children watch TV through Youtube. Companies spend large sums of money on banner advertising. News stations need to re-invent the way they broadcast news. The news reporter of today is the person with a mobile phone who is personally affected by the news event, posting a video on Youtube. For global news events or global disasters, the real newsgathering takes place on Youtube, Twitter or Facebook, delivered by the people who are actually affected by the incidents.

Let me put Social Media in the right context for you. Digital marketing buys you online and offline coverage through pay-per-click advertising. Social Media earns you online and offline coverage. It is all about online reputation. By being on Social Media networks you engage with your customers in their world. They no longer go to your web site. They expect you to come to theirs. On Facebook, on LinkedIn or on Twitter. By sharing good content with them in their world, they want to know more about you. Through Social Media, you drive people to your web site thereby creating prospects and building relationships.

Once they are on your website, you convert them into a sale or a lead by having call to actions in place. "Click here to buy", "Click here to download our whitepaper" or "Click here to register for our event". Once they click you have the opportunity to take their details and enter into the sales cycle with them.

When you have converted the relationship into a sale, Social Media allows you to hang on to the customer relationship. You are taking the offline relationship into the online world. By regularly sharing good content with them you are raising your credibility and your expertise with the customer. This can lead to two things: First, they buy from you again if they need more of your products; and second, they will recommend you to their friends.

Consider your website as your castle. You serve your home market through your castle. But not everybody lives in your country. Some live in Facebook land. Some live in Twitter land. To reach them you are going to set up a presence in those countries. These are your embassies. By sharing good content in your embassies you will build a loyal community and they might be interested in visiting your castle. To find out more about what you have to offer. But there are other people out there who live in other countries. It is too expensive to open embassies in all those countries. So for these countries you create outposts. These could be for Youtube or Slideshare. From these outposts you are going to throw out snippets of your content. We call this link bait. So you create as many outposts as possible to drive people to your embassies. From your embassies, you lead them to your castle because that's where you want to do the ultimate transaction with them.

Social Media myths

Social Media is free. Many of the Social Media networks and tools are free. Some of them monetise their business by offering a premium service as well. But what is not free is your time. And time is money. Doing your Social Media takes time. You need a number of hours each week to spend on developing your Social Media and online reputation by listening online, creating and sharing content and growing your communities.

Social Media will give your business an immediate boost. It takes time to see measurable results from social media. It takes dedication, consistency and repetition of your key message. It needs to grow and the more content you share, the faster your reputation will grow. Ultimately, you will see that leads come in through your Social Media. Plan on limited monetisation for at least six to twelve months.

Your numbers of fans or followers matters. There are places on the web where you can buy 5,000 Twitter followers for $5. But they can't guarantee you quality for this. And it is the quality not the quantity that's important. It is better to have followers that are engaged with your brand rather than just having a big number of followers or likes on your site.

If you build it, they will come. Many businesses think that when they are on Facebook engagement will happen automatically. That's not how it happens. You need to promote and drive traffic to your Social Media sites by sharing good content and pro-actively engage with your followers.

Social Media isn't measurable. Social Media is marketing delight. Every aspect of what you do in Social Media is measurable. There are tools to measure traffic, engagement, sentiments and Return On Investment (ROI).

Social Media replaces all other marketing channels. People still watch TV. People still visit web sites. E-mail is still being used. Social Media is another communication channel. The best social media campaigns leverage social media, web site, TV and public relations. But where traditional marketing channels are often used in isolation, social media has a much bigger impact on the way a business operates and is being perceived in the market.

Social Media truths

The truth is that your customers are using Social Media with or without your participation. You can ignore it, but they will still talk about you. They will make buying decisions, and they do it with or without you. If you are not there, they move on engage with your competitors who are there.

Another truth is that Social Media content is permanent. Once it is out there, people can share it. They can download it. It is permanent. Companies are now checking Facebook profiles of people they intend to recruit. Social Media can hurt and it can help you. Companies have lost market valuation in an instant by not listening to what their customers were talking about. On the other hand, companies can increase customer satisfaction by immediately responding to customer requests on social media.

If you decide to start using social media for your business you are faced with a multitude of social networks and tools to choose from, each with their own characteristics, functionalities and target groups. They differ per market, per region, per sector, per industry, per skill set. For many people, this is where they get scared and they say: "OMG, where do I start"?

Fortunately, It is not that complicated. In the next chapter I will try to put some order in this chaos.

THE SOCIAL MEDIA LANDSCAPE

Choosing the right social media networks and tools is a key element of your strategy. There is a wide variety to choose from, and tools you pick today may be obsolete tomorrow. In this chapter we will give you an overview of different options you have. They are:

- Social Networks
- Blogs
- Microblogs
- Social Bookmarking
- Video and photo Sharing
- Forums
- Reviews and Opinions
- Article Sharing
- Presentation Sharing
- Podcasts
- Wikis

Social Networks

The first group is social networking sites. The leading ones are Facebook, LinkedIn and Google+. They come and go. Myspace was bigger than Facebook when it started but they are now a small niche Social Media network targeting music and bands. Bebo was very popular with teenagers, more popular than Facebook. In a matter of 2 years they disappeared and all teenagers moved to Facebook. Social Networking sites all work according to the same concepts. You sign up, you create your online profile and you connect with likeminded people: in Facebook they are called your friends; in LinkedIn they are your connections. Then you start sharing content with your connections. They all offer additional apps (applications) to enrich the user experience and drive additional engagement. In Facebook you can chat and play games. On LinkedIn, you can join discussion groups. On Google+, there is Google Hangouts for video conferencing. But they all work according to the same concepts. Ultimately it all comes down to sharing relevant content. By sharing content, you grow your online reputation. All social network providers saw the potential for businesses. If they could somehow give businesses access to their members, they could start monetising their social network. So they all allow businesses to create a company page. People can then connect with the company's page and from then on these people would see the company updates on their home feed.

Blogs

My recommendation to most of my clients is that if you want to start with Social Media, start blogging. Why? Because with a blog, you start creating content. A blog is short for web log. It is an online diary. It is a website that you can create with a push of a button and you can maintain easily by adding regular entries in the form of commentary, description of an event, a review, an idea or a suggestion. Blogs are inherently viral. You add links, photos, and video. Then you send out notifications on the web, "Click here to read my latest blog post about..." A very powerful social networking tool to drive traffic to your web site. There are big businesses built around blogs. One of the biggest blogs in Social Media is Mashable.com. A guy in Scotland started his blog on Social Media and it is now a million-dollar business. The Huffington Post is a big business built around blogs covering many different topics. So blogging is one of the most powerful aspects of Social Media for the simple reason that it is the easiest way to start creating your own content.

Microblogs

Microblogs are like blogs, but they are shorter. Twitter is a microblog. Only 140 characters. Microblogs enable people to post thoughts about a topic or an idea, but on a much smaller scale. It could be a short sentence. They are they are even more viral than a blog. You can add a photo, a link, a video. Through these short messages, you can direct people to other places on the web, direct them to your blog, direct them to your Facebook page or to your website. So they are really good direction agents to other content on the web. Many tweets have a link to a photo or a video. But Twitter is not the only microblog. Tumblr is a powerful blogging platform used by designers to share their creative work.

Social Bookmarking

Social bookmarking is another category of social media tool. You may have heard of web sites like Delicious, Digg, reddit, AddThis. But not many people understand what you can do with them. Social bookmarking is a simple concept. If you like a website, you add it to your favourites on your desktop on your browser. So if you change your browser, or if you change your desktop or your laptop, you will lose all your favourite bookmarks. So why not bookmark these sites online? Go to a site like Delicious, register, create your profile and then instead of bookmarking your favourite sites on your desktop, you bookmark them in your private section in Delicious. The biggest immediate advantage for you is, wherever you are in the world, whatever PC you are using, whatever browser you are using, you will always have access to your favourite bookmarks.

But here is the real benefit. Since your bookmarks are now online, you can also share them with other people. You can share your favourite bookmarks with your customers or with your colleagues. This is where social bookmarking becomes a very productive tool. People nowadays go to sites like Delicious to search for good content. Instead of having those search results from the Google Search robots, you now get search results in Delicious from experts who have bookmarked their favourite sites. Make sure you get a few social bookmarking icons on your web site so people can bookmark your site easily on sites like Delicious, StumbleUpon or Digg.

Video and Photo Sharing

The growth of Social Media is being driven by video and photo sharing. Photo sharing is the number one feature on Facebook. Sharing video is what makes Youtube what it is today. It is about emotion, immediacy and visualisation of your content. Through sites like Youtube, Flickr or Vimeo, you can share and distribute video clips and photos. You can create branded channels on Youtube or Vimeo to help you generate additional brand exposure.

Forums

Forums are online message boards and discussion sites where users gather to discuss topics or subjects. There are hundreds of topics on the web that people talk about. Usually, there is a moderator that sets the guidelines for the forums. LinkedIn Groups are forums as well. Gaming Companies have forums for their games where children chat about the games and play the games online with other friends around the world. These are big forums and there are many people within those gaming companies monitoring these forums to make sure that everybody is there for genuine reasons.

Reviews and Opinions

Key engagement drivers in Social Media are review and opinion sites. People love to share their opinions. They share the experiences they had with a hotel, a shop or a concert. Who hasn't booked a hotel through TripAdvisor? Sites like Google Local, Yahoo Local and Yelp now offer businesses the opportunity to promote their business locally and get reviews and star ratings from their clients. These sites are very important to get conversations around your business and to drive traffic to your Social Media sites or your website.

Article Sharing

Article sharing is about repurposing your content. You do that through article-distribution sites like Squidoo. On these sites you upload your articles, e-books, white papers etc. People go to article sharing sites to search for articles on every topic that you can imagine. Each article includes a slug line, a description of the author and a link to the site. A great place to create outposts to drive traffic to your web site.

Presentation Sharing

SlideShare, owned by LinkedIn, is a community on the web where people share PowerPoint presentations, either in PDF or PowerPoint format. People share knowledge and ideas and it is a great source for generating business leads. You can turn a blog post into a set of slides and upload it on SlideShare. Many people search on Slideshare for good content. If you have the right keywords and description, your presentation will come up in the search results. It will drive traffic back to your web site. It is all about sharing your content, repurposing your content and about being seen on as many places as possible. With a premium account you can capture people's contact details before they can download your presentations.

Podcasts

A podcast is a digital media file (audio or video) that is downloaded directly from a streaming Internet source. It is a combination of the words iPod and Broadcast. Podcasts are distributed on the Internet using syndication feeds, or podcasting websites, and are hosted or authored by a podcaster. The media files are downloaded onto a computer, your smart phone or an iPod. Many people simplify the podcast definition simply by calling it an online, prerecorded radio program over the Internet.

Wikis

Wikis are websites that allow you to easily collaborate,

create and edit information on a certain topic. Organisations use internal wikis to capture best practices or and ideas. People collaborate to enhance and rate the wiki content. A track record is kept of all the changes. A wiki can become a living organism of linked content in an organisation.

FOCUS

"You can't depend on your eyes when your imagination is out of focus".

Mark Twain

Strategy is all about focus. If you haven't got a clear, specific Social Media strategy, you cannot measure your success. You need to set very clear objectives on what you want to achieve with your Social Media.

One of the key challenges that you will face in setting your strategy is the nature of your executive's point-of-view towards Social Media. It could well be that your executive team may be hesitant towards Social Media, that they don't believe in Social Media. Many executives have the same position: If it doesn't make us money, then why would we invest in this? What is the Return on investment (ROI)? Prove that we can make money or save cost through social and then we will consider putting resources into Social Media.

This reservation towards Social Media, is often based on three factors.

1.   First, senior management may be afraid of losing control. Many executives say: "What if customers start talking negative about us? If a negative story starts spreading we lose control." Your counter argument is that negative comments may happen anyway. And when they happen it is better to participate in these conversations. By participating you have a chance to direct the conversation and address the concerns that are being discussed. The beauty of Social Media lies in the fact that it is open and transparent. It is a great opportunity to listen to what your stakeholders have to say.

2.   Executives may be hesitant because they don't understand what Social Media can do for them. In this case you have to make clear to senior management that although Social Media is driven by the younger generation, they are the decision-makers of tomorrow. If you want to inspire new leaders in your organisation, then you have to be open as an organisation and have to be using Social Media. Otherwise, you will not get those people to join your company. Management often doesn't understand what they can do with Social Media. They hear about it from their children but they haven't necessarily made the link to what it can do for their business. It is this lack of understanding that needs to be addressed.

3.   Finally, many executives still think that social media is a fad. Social Media will go away. It is a hype and the hype will slowly make sense for commonsense. Therefore, they don't want to invest in social media. The usage numbers show that Social Media is not a hype and is here to stay. Socialbakers.com is a website that will give you very good usage statistics of Social Media sites like Facebook, Linkedin and Twitter.

If your executive team is not in favour of Social Media you have to address this first. Make sure they understand the openness of Social Media and the fact that they won't be losing control. In fact, they will be gaining control in the conversations. Make sure they understand all the ins and outs of Social Media, and what you can achieve with it. Make sure they understand that this is something that is fundamentally changing the way businesses and the world operate. It can be very useful to find an ally in the executive team who you can use as a sponsor in converting the other members of the management team. Convince them that Social Media is something that the company must invest in by showing them tangible benefits.

A book that can give you additional arguments for your discussions with management is The Cluetrain Manifesto. The Cluetrain Manifesto is a set of 95 theses organised and put forward as a manifesto, or call to action, for all businesses operating within what is suggested to be a newly connected marketplace. The manifesto was written in 1999 by Rick Levine, Christopher Locke, Doc Searls, and David Weinberger. Today, the statements are even more powerful than they were fourteen years ago. Here are some of the statements:

"A powerful global conversation has begun. Through the Internet, people are discovering and inventing new ways to share relevant knowledge with blinding speeds. As a direct result, markets are getting smarter and getting smarter faster than most companies."

"These markets are conversations. They are members communicating language that is natural, open, honest, direct, funny and often shocking. Whether they are explaining or complaining, joking or serious, the human voice is unmistakably genuine. It can't be faked."

"In the old world, most companies only know how to talk in the soothing, humorless monotone of the mission statement, marketing brochure – "Your call is important to us…" busy signal. No wonder network markets have no respect for companies unable or unwilling to speak as they do."

There are still too many businesses behaving and talking old world style. Examples can be found when you have a problem with your telephone provider, or with your bank. When you call them, the first thing you will hear is, "Your call is important to us…" If you can find the telephone number on their website. In the new world, you expect them to be on Twitter or that you can go to their Facebook page, and connect with them on your territory. They better be there because if they are not, you will move on.

What is Social Media NOT for business?

- It is not a bulletin board for marketing and PR.
- It is not a cheap way of advertising.
- It is not one-sided.
- It is not about self-promotion.
- It is not to talk negative about other people or about your competitors.
- It is not the only way to market your business.
- It is not the answer to all your prayers.

What is Social Media for business?

- It is word of mouth on steroids. You can get the word out in blinding speed on a global scale.
- It is a Brand awareness multiplier. A great tool to create (viral) awareness around your brand.
- It is a new lead generation tool. It is really good to find new people willing to do business with you.
- It is a great tool to measure customer satisfaction and to improve it.

- It is a tool that can give you ideas and insights to improve your business.
- It helps you refine your positioning.
- It is a new recruitment channel.
- It is a global and immediate news broadcaster.
- It helps you in building your communities.

I have been saying for some time now that Social Media is the biggest change in business I have seen in my corporate career. Here is why:

1. Business is changing from selling to connecting with an audience. No longer do brands dictate people in anonymous markets what to buy. But it is the brand that builds relationships by connecting, communicating and interacting with their target audiences. Making sure that the right person gets the right product at the right time.

2. Marketing is changing from large campaigns to small acts. No longer do you have to communicate one uniform message to anonymous targets and market segments. But now, it is small acts to individual groups of people within specific market segments. This is very powerful. You can now advertise on Facebook and target men between 20 and 25 years, living in London who are passionate about golf.

3. It is from controlling the message to being transparent. No longer can you tell the audience what to do. And no longer can you expect your audience to listen to what you have to say. You need to listen to them and tailor your message. Make your message transparent by listening and responding to them.

4. From being hard to reach to being available everywhere. Instead of you expecting your

customers to come to your website to connect with you, you go to the places where they are. On Facebook, LinkedIn or on Twitter. And if they like your attitude and behaviour they will connect with you.

This is a generational change. This will take 10-20 years to change the way businesses go about growing their business. The younger generation of today who live and breathe Social Media will be the decision makers of tomorrow. For them this is business as usual. It is a fundamental change. It is changing from a closed, controlled and intuitive business approach to one of being open, random and networked.

Social Media Return on Investment (ROI)

Social Media ROI can be found in many places. It is about unlocking productivity in your organisation. You can work faster, you can work smarter and you can share content within your organisation. These are powerful benefits you can get from Social Media. You can work faster in getting lead-generation campaigns out to the market. You can work smarter by having conversations with your target market, understanding exactly what their requirements are and tailoring your message towards them.

From an ROI point of view this will lead to cost savings. You can reduce email within your organisation thereby reducing your cost of IT and gaining more productive hours in the organisation. You can complete internal processes faster by sharing documents online.

It is about unlocking money in your organisation. By listening on the web, you can find leads. By publishing your own content, like your own blog, you can grow your community and therefore, getting in contact with new people who are willing to do business with you. By engaging in conversations, you get a better understanding of your customer's needs. You can build relationships with your customers so they will come back and buy again.

From an ROI point of view this will lead to increase in revenue. Social Media will give you an additional sales channel. You can target more specific markets, giving you a better lead to sales conversion ratio and ensuring your sales people work on those leads with the highest closing ratio. And you will increase lifetime revenue from existing clients because you are developing not only your offline but now also your online relationships with your customers.

Another major ROI factor in this area is the reduction of your marketing cost. A lot of the Social Media channels are free and much more targeted. Which means you can save money on more general marketing activities like advertising, events and creating traditional marketing collateral.

It is about unlocking potential in your organisation. You can use Social Media to innovate, develop your internal culture and use Social Media to make your employees into brand ambassadors.

From an ROI point of view this means that Social Media can help you reduce your recruitment costs. By having an engaged workforce you will also lower your staff attrition rates which means that investments you do in your employees will not get lost.

Why do businesses use Social Media?

1. Businesses use Social Media for brand awareness and recognition. Whether you are a consumer-brand or a business-to-business brand, it is about getting people to engage with your brand.

2. Businesses use it for improving customer service. They use Social Media to respond quicker to customer requirements. If you offer your service on the social channels that your customers are on (i.e. Twitter or Facebook) you can work much more effectively in responding to their requests.

3. Businesses use Social Media to develop themselves as experts in their market by offering their customers valuable content. They see their content no longer as a proprietary asset. As a Social Media consultant once told me: "Social Media is all about sharing your content and selling your expertise". More and more businesses use Social Media to share information and knowledge to stand out from their competitors.

4. More and more businesses start seeing the power of Social Media in generating additional revenues. Sales people can benefit from Social Media by listening on Twitter or Google+ to find leads. Local businesses can find new customers with money to spend by combining social, mobile and local online tools. Giving businesses the opportunity to target local customers and giving their customers the opportunity to rate their sales experience they have when they bought the product or service.

How much time should I spend on Social Media?

A key question many people ask me when they attend my workshops is how much time to spend on Social Media. My standard answer to this question is always the same: "How much time do you spend on e-mail?" You will be surprised to hear that the minimum time they spend on e-mail is anywhere between two and three hours a day. I then ask them, "You don't have time to do your social media but you do have time to spend two, three hours a day on e-mail?" They then realise that it becomes a different type of question. Not about how much time should I spend on Social Media, but how can Social Media help me win time by doing things more efficient.

Email is the most interruptive piece of office software that's out there. People respond to it when they hear e-mails coming in. Half of the e-mails you are cc'ed on and they are not relevant. People also spend a lot of time in organising their e-mail box. Try to get out of your mailbox for half an hour a day and use that half hour on Social Media. You will see massive, massive results from that. It far outweighs the time that you lose on your e-mail.

Tools versus strategy

Many businesses fall into the trap of going straight into setting up their social media networks and tools. They skip strategising and planning their social media. Many of them end up not knowing what to tweet about or posting boring content on their Facebook page. Don't rush to start using the tools. Develop your Social Media strategy, integrate it with your marketing plan and make sure you've got the resources available to execute your Social Media strategy.

Your Social Media strategy

Businesses use Social Media to generate exposure for their business, to improve traffic to their websites, to develop themselves as a thought leader, to establish new partnerships, to generate leads, to improve SEO for their website or to improve customer satisfaction. Those are measureable goals and you can set Key Performance Indicators (KPIs) against each of them.

Here are the key components of your Social Media strategy.

- Your purpose. Why are you doing Social Media?
- Customer analysis. You need to know where your customers are, on what networks they hang out and what they talk about.
- Content strategy. What content and when are you going to publish
- Your online brand personality
- Your niche: How unique are you? The more unique Social Media, the easier it will be to generate your content.
- The tools you will be using to manage your Social Media.
- The internal and external processes for your Social Media. Who is writing the blog post? Is there an approval cycle, etc?
- Measurement of your Social Media activities, engagement and sentiment

There are three aspects of your Social Media strategy that I want to highlight. Personas, Positioning and Keywords.

Personas

Personas are archetypal characters created to represent the different user types within your market that might use your site, brand or product a similar way. Personas are a way to consider the goals, desires and limitations of your customers. They are used to guide decisions about your messaging and content strategy.

Marketing personas are not a single user. They are a representation of the goals and behaviors of a fictional group of users. In many cases they are captured in a 1-2 page description that include behavior patterns, goals, skills, attitudes, and a few fictional details the make the persona a realistic character.

Here are two simple examples for a music publisher selling music clips and sheet music to a business audience.

Persona 1 – John: George is a 45 year old violin teacher who has used the Internet for less than a year. He accesses the Internet from home over a broadband connection. He has never purchased online before, preferring to place orders by phone.

Persona 2 – Jill: Georgina is a 29 year old ad exec who has been using the Internet for 5 years and uses her Macbook, iPad or Android phone to access the web – whatever is to hand.

You can see that these are quite different types of people who will have quite different needs. Some companies simply use personas at this level. True personas have a more detailed narrative and summary of customer goals and characteristics.

Benefits of personas

- Using personas will help you to build consistency across the business for your marketing messages.
- Personas will guide you in better understanding of your customer's needs.
- Understanding where your customers are spending their time will enable better targeting of your social media content.
- You can do more targeted analytics as you can discover which types of personas make better customers.

Positioning

You need to make sure that you are unique in the way you position yourself, not only as your company, but also in your Social Media. The more unique you are, the easier it will be to generate content. The more passionate you are about your positioning, the easier it will be for you to create your content to help you drive your Social Media engagement.

If you can change or refresh your company positioning, then this is where you should start when you develop your Social Media strategy. It could well be that you are not in a position to change the company positioning. Then you need to do this postioning exercise for your Social Media. What messages are you going to focus on with your Social Media?

A very good tool in developing your positioning statement is to create your elevator pitch. The elevator test is a simple formula that I borrowed from Geoffrey Moore in his book Crossing the Chasm:

For companies A, B, C,

Who need .....

Our product/service is (your category) .....

That does (your features) ......

Unlike competitors A-B-C

My product/service differentiators are .....

Here is an example positioning statement for a company that sells backpacks:

For international travelers
Who are tired of the shortcomings of large-capacity backpacks,
The Tortuga is a travel backpack
That provides the security and easy access travelers need.
Unlike hiking backpacks
The Tortuga is designed specifically for urban travel.

If you follow this format, you will get a very powerful statement that you can use as the basis for your positioning and as the basis for your Social Media. You can give that to your copywriter and use it as the building blocks of your marketing messages.

Keywords

The advantage of creating a positioning statement is that it will also give you your keywords. They are the basis of your online strategy. If you want to get high search engine rankings keywords play an important role. From a marketing perspective they are important as well. They help you to develop your content and build your reputation. The more often you use them and the better you use them in the titles of your blog posts, in your blog posts, in the titles of your profiles and on your website, the more people will associate your company with your keywords. This will give you a preferential brain position when they need to make a purchase decision. It is therefore very important that you understand the "keyword universe" for your business.

Don't go for the obvious, usually shorter keywords. One of the most expensive keywords in Google is "insurance". If you want to run a Google Adwords campaign on the word "insurance", you have to pay a lot per click. Try to start with the so-called long-tail terms. So instead of "insurance", you are going to go for "farmers insurance" or "insurance for young families". So start with accessible, cheaper long-tailed terms and then build towards more generic terms over time.

There are many tools available on the web that can help you in analysing and testing your keywords. "Google Suggest" will suggest keywords when you enter your search terms. "Google AdWords" has a keyword tool in which you can compare keywords and analyse the costs and competition if you would advertise with them.

LISTENING

"Knowledge speaks, but wisdom listens."
Jimi Hendrix

Thanks to the technologies that power Social Media, it is now possible to listen online to whatever you want to listen to. Whether you want to listen to your customers, news, opinions, music, celebrities, somewhere on the web there will be the exact piece of content that will satisfy your requirement. The challenge of listening is not the actual act of listening, but the process of filtering the information so you get the content you need. Online listening gives a whole new dimension to what brands can do online, what they can learn online and how they can use that knowledge to their advantage.

When you listen online you learn. You learn about what is happening in your market. You learn about what is happening in your business ecosystem: your customers, your partners and even your employees. It is about finding out what they have to say, and then collaborate internally and externally to address the issues that people are talking about or dealing with the opportunities that you will find.

By listening online to what people are saying about your company, or about your products, you are able to protect your brand's image. Branding has changed dramatically with the emergence of Social Media. It is being turned upside down. I call this reversed branding. Branding is no longer you telling your customers what to read, where to read or where to view what you have to say to them. But nowadays it is about your customers telling you where to connect and where to communicate with them. By listening online to your customers, you know exactly what their perception is of your brand, how they feel about your brand and whether they are positive or negative about your brand.

By listening online, you can also identify, mitigate and manage potential crisis situations. You can avert a crisis or turn a crisis into an opportunity. By listening online you can respond adequately if there are issues that people talk about. Blackberry experienced this when they did not listen online to what people were saying about the Blackberry Messenger service problems they experienced a few years ago. Since then, their brand and market valuation have gone in a steep decline. O^2 in the UK experienced a similar service failure and listened carefully on Twitter. They responded to every tweet in a conversational style. They turned it from a potential crisis into an opportunity in showing the industry how to use Social Media correctly in times of a crisis.

Why listen online

There are plenty of reasons why you should listen online. By listening, you learn about your customers. You learn about what they think and how they use your product. You get a better understanding of what they need. You find out what people are saying about your brand, if it is positive or negative. And it will also allow you to identify the people who talk most about your company and/or products. They could well be key influencers for you.

When you listen properly and you respond to what is being said about product issues or product questions, you can increase customer satisfaction. Companies are using Social Media tools to listen to their clients and offer them a channel to talk about product or service issues.

Listening can also help you to assess the performance of your products. By listening on discussion groups or forums about what people are saying about your products, you can learn about the issues, what works, what doesn't work, what features are appreciated, what features are not appreciated.

You can listen to yourself, to your market or to your trends. You can also listen to your competitors. You get a better understanding of them and you can track their announcements. You can better anticipate and respond to what they are doing in your market.

You can identify the sentiment, or the tone of voice of what people are talking about. Is it positive or is it negative? For big brands this is a key source of information that can help them in the development and implementation of the right marketing campaigns for the right people in the right market. It allows them to address local cultural characteristics.

Big consumer brands listen to their customers every day. It is vital that they listen online to what people say about their products. How they use it, are there problems, who are the most vocal etc. Many of these companies have a global Social Media listening center. A central room with large screens, showing various listening dashboards. They can see exactly what people are saying, who the key influences are, who is positive, who is negative. Gaming companies are constantly listening in on the discussion groups of the children who are playing their games just to make sure that everybody who is on those groups are there for genuine reasons.

Listening online gives salespeople a new channel for lead generation. By listening they can find out if people need their products or services or if they need more general advice. Twitter, LinkedIn and Google+ are great networks to search for leads. By searching properly, you can find leads that could be relevant. You don't respond to those leads in a sales mode (click here to buy), but you engage in the conversation. You build up a relationship and you can slowly turn that relationship into a sales opportunity.

Your listening strategy

So what is your strategy for listening? Besides listening online to fine-tune your Social Media strategy.

Listen to find your customers online. The first stage of your listening strategy is that you need to determine where your customers are. What social networks do they use? Or in Social Media terms: who are the tribes and where do they hang out?

Listen to find your influencers. The second part of your Social Media listening strategy is to find the key influences for your business. Today's new influencers are the bloggers. Businesses now launch new products by bringing together the top bloggers about their products or industry, online or offline, and brief them on the new product or the new service. They then start blogging about it and coverage will be created immediately. It is no longer about column inches ("old style" PR) but it's about page impressions. And of course, when you know your key bloggers, you can also start building relationships with them. You can invite them to be a guest blogger on your blog, or you can refer to them on your web site.

Listen to your customers and your competitors. It is really useful to listen online to what your clients and what your competitors are saying. You might find new sales opportunities or you can pick up potential crisis situations when people start talking about problems they have with your competitor. Identify the online forums and the LinkedIn groups that your customers are using so you can listen learn and engage.

Listen to your keywords and hashtags. A very important aspect of your listening is to listen to the keywords of your business, the hashtags and the trends. By doing this you will find opportunities, issues and inspirational content that you can use for your blog. But most important of all, you can find news and trends that you can leverage for the execution of your Social Media and content strategy

Where are the tribes?

In social media terms, your customers are your tribes. And you want to know where they hang out. To find out which social networks your customers are using you need to have a basic understanding of what each social network has to offer. That brings us to a high-level introduction of the various Social Media networks.

Facebook is the biggest social network. It has over a billion registered users. Facebook continues to evolve for businesses through advanced distribution and targeting options. More and more people are getting worried about the privacy in Facebook. There is increased pressure on Facebook to monetise their business. They now advertise on your Facebook home page, in your news feed and even on your mobile Facebook app.

If you would summarise the essence of Facebook, it would be "where every moment lives for eternity". It is about sharing the moment. About sharing what people are passionate about. That's why brands with many fans, most likely consumer brands, are more successful on Facebook than business brands. If you are a consumer brand, if lots of people talk about your brand or if there is a lot of passion around your brand you should definitely be on Facebook.

Twitter is a key social network for marketers. They can monitor conversations and learn about their customers. Or they can use Twitter to distribute content and build relationships with people. Growth is stable and businesses are making money with Twitter. It is one of the hottest tools for businesses right now.

Twitter is about now. It is for those instances when few

words can say a lot. It is instant. It is immediate. It is for celebrities to keep their fans up to date on what they are doing, every minute of the day. It is for businesses to share content and direct people to relevant places on the web. It is a great tool to search for the latest news on any topic, as well for business as for general news. If you have instant news that you want to communicate to your market or if you want to drive people to your web site through "link bait", Twitter is a must.

LinkedIn is a major social workhorse for marketing and sales teams across the world. Everything is inextricably linked to business. It is Facebook with a tie. In Facebook you are worried about your privacy settings. In LinkedIn you want people to know everything there is about you, as long as it relates to your professional life. LinkedIn is for your personal career and for developing your company's online reputation. That's why LinkedIn is more appropriate for business-to-business companies. LinkedIn has undergone many changes over the last year. It had a facelift, it added analytics and it has really strengthened its position.

Google+ is now the second-biggest social network. They've added an amazing array of features. Their main proposition is that if you really want to maximize your SEO (Search Engine Optimization), then Google+ is a must. Google+ is Google's social layer over all the Google products whether it is Youtube, Google Mail, Google Drive etc. Google+ is really good for businesses that want to target their audiences through segmentation. Google+ allows you to do that like no other social network can. Google+ is set to be one of the key networks that you need to take into consideration as a marketer.

Pinterest is one of the fastest-growing Social Media networks out there. It is the new kid on the block.

Particularly popular among women. It allows you to bookmark all the beautiful photos and videos you find on the web on pinboards and then share these with your followers or anybody else who finds it on Pinterest. It drives traffic to your website if you use it properly. Retail businesses create beautiful pinboards of their catalogue and by doing this use Pinterest as another channel to drive people to their web site or online catalogue.

Instagram is an online photo-sharing, video-sharing and social networking service that enables users to take pictures and videos, apply digital filters to them, and share them on a variety of social networking services, such as Facebook, Twitter, Tumblr and Flickr.

More and more businesses start to approach Instagram as a full-blown social media network, particularly if their business is very visual and they are targeting a younger and smart phone active audience.

If I want to summarize the above on its highest level: Facebook is for consumers; Twitter is a broadcasting and communication tool to keep in touch with your customers in-between your blog posts; LinkedIn is for B2B; Google+ is to optimise your SEO and for targeting a slightly more professional audience. Pinterest is great when you target women and can visualise your product in inspirational environments. Instagram is when you target a younger, mobile aware audience who live for the moment and want to capture and share these moments as a photographer.

It is also important to consider which countries across the world world you are targeting. Social Media in China is huge and the social network landscape is completely different. Facebook, Twitter, Google or Youtube are not allowed in China. So they created their own Social Media networks. LinkedIn is very strong in the US, UK, Brazil and India. Google+ and Pinterest are not strong in the Middle East but Instagram is.

Don't forget local and bespoke Social Media networks. If you are targeting women with children, there is Mumsnet.com. If you are targeting a retired audience, there is olderiswiser.com. There are different Social Media networks for different target groups. You also need to be aware of local networks like mumsnet.com or olderiswiser.com. These are social networks with the same characteristics as Facebook and LinkedIn. They target a different or a local audience. It is another place where your customers can hang out.

Finding your key influencers

Bloggers are the new influencers. People no longer go to price-comparison websites or to companies' websites. They check out bloggers. They are the specialists in a particular area so that's where people can find independent knowledge about the product they want to buy. It is key that you know the top 10 bloggers of your industry.

How do you find your favourite bloggers? It is a skill. You really need to spend a number of hours searching on the web to find those bloggers. Start your search on blog search engines and then you dig deeper and deeper. You will find more and more links to bloggers that are relevant. Always check the post date of their latest blog post. If the latest blog post was done a year ago, it is probably a blogger that is no longer active.

The first place you can go to is Technorati.com. Technorati is the global directory of blogs. On this site you can search for blogs or blog posts. When you've done a search, you get a listing of the relevant bloggers that are registered in Technorati. The higher the reputation of that blogger in Technorati, the higher he or she will show up in the listing. Check the description and if you like what you read you go to their website. You read the blog and when you like the blog you bookmark it. Tag the blog with "My Favorite Blogs" so you can easily find the blog again when you add it to your online listening station.

One of the best places to search for blogs is Google Blog Search. There are many services in Google that people are not aware of and one of those services is Google Blog Search. By going to google.com/blogsearch, Google will only list blogs or blog posts for the term you searched on.

With social bookmarking becoming more and more important for search you can also search for bloggers in bookmarking sites like Delicious. Make sure you add the word "blog" to your search term.

Twitter is also a good place to find bloggers. Often, people put in their Twitter profile (their Twitter bio) that they blog about a certain subject. Followerwonk.com is a site where you can search for Twitter bios and the good thing about searching here is that it also gives you an influence rating for the blogger.

Once you've found a blogger that seems interesting, check the following:

- When was the last blog post?
- Are the articles interesting?
- Does it give me what I need?
- Do they refer to other bloggers in their blog posts?
- Do they have a blog roll?

Good bloggers often have a blog roll on their website. This is a list of the favourite bloggers of the blogger. Blogs they want to share with their readers. When you like a particular blog, then you will probably also like the blogs from their blog roll. Often, this is a great source of good bloggers that you can start following.

Plenty of ways to find your favourite bloggers, but it is a bit of a skill. You go from site to site and dig deeper and deeper into the blogosphere. If you are lost, you can always search in Google for "the top 10 bloggers in (your location) about (your topic). You will be surprised with the search results.

Listen to keywords, hashtags, customers and competitors

The next thing you need to do is listening to your keywords, hastags, customers and competitors. By setting up alerts for your keywords you will get notifications every time the word shows up somewhere new on the Internet. The best tool for setting alerts is Google Alerts. In Google Alerts, you can set alerts on words. Those can be your online keywords. It can be your company name. It can be your CEO's name. It can be your competitor's name. As soon as new content emerges on the web and Google picks it up, Google Alerts will then give you an alert via an e-mail or via RSS.

RSS (Rich Site Summary)

RSS (It is also referred to as Really Simple Syndication) is a format for delivering regularly changing web content. Many news-related sites, weblogs and other online publishers syndicate their content as an RSS Feed to whoever wants it. It allows you to easily stay informed by retrieving the latest content from the sites you are interested in. You save time by not needing to visit each site individually.

Listen to trends

In Google Trends you can search for words or topics and see how popular these terms are over time and by location. It also gives you related keywords and subjects.

You can also listen in Google Insights. All the search data Google collects is being made available in various formats through Google Insights. It can give you insights in where people search, how they search, what they search for, what the trends are. You can search this database by market, by gender etc. You can even create you own infographics in Google Insights.

It is important to look for trends in Twitter and Youtube. These trends are key drivers for Social Media engagement. What are the trending topics on Twitter? What are the hottest videos that people are watching? What are the most popular photos that are being shared? When you know the type of videos that are being watched at the moment, you can take that into consideration with your own content creation.

Listen to news

You can listen to news on news websites like BBC or CNN. It is important to listen to news sites so you can relate your content to the things that are happening in the world around you. This will increase the chance that people will engage with your content. A great tool for listening to news is newsmap.jp. This is an application that visually

FLIRTONOMICS

reflects the constantly changing landscape of the Google News aggregator.

Your online listening station

Instead of having to go to all those websites to listen and to stay up to date, you want to let those web sites come to you. That's what your online listening station will do for you. By subscribing to the RSS feeds of your favourite bloggers, your alerts, your news sites etc. you can embed their updates in your own listening station. Any update on the source web site will automatically be updated on your listening station. This is where the real power of online listening comes in. By bringing all your listening elements into one dashboard, you can be very effective in staying up to date.

When I come into my office in the morning, instead of switching on my e-mail, I switch on my online listening station. I listen to what is happening on my social networks and what new articles my favourite bloggers have published overnight. It gives me an overview of what my customers are talking about and what my competitors have announced. I get an update of the latest news in my market, my region, my country and the world. And if I'm lucky I may have picked up one or two business leads. This is much more valuable to me than scanning through dozens of e-mails with half of them being irrelevant or spam.

There are different versions of an online listening station. A very simple one is what I call your open listening station. Without having to register for any website, you can go to Topsy.com and search for people or subjects on the web, or filter by blog, discussion boards, Twitter etc.

But the best listening stations are your personal online listening station. My favourite tool is Netvibes. With Netvibes you create multiple tabs in your listening dashboard. The first tab is your own Social Media networks. You see exactly what is happening on your social networks. You then have a tab with your favourite Social Media blogs, a tab with your favourite news sites and a tab with specific search terms that you specified. By clicking through these tabs each morning, you stay up to date. In 20 minutes I'm fully up to date with what is happening in my world.

INTEGRATION

"The more connections that can be made in the brain, the more integrated the experience is within memory."

Don Campbell

Now that you know where your clients are you are going to set up your Facebook, LinkedIn, Twitter, Youtube, or whatever social network is relevant to engage with your clients. You are going to set up your embassies and your outposts and create an integrated environment where you can easily spread content from your castle to your embassies and repurpose this content through your outposts. In this chapter I will give you a more detailed overview of how your business can benefit from Facebook, Twitter, LinkedIn, Google+, Youtube, Pinterest and Instagram. I will also show you how to optimise your pages on those social networks and I will give you guidance on how to grow your networks of friends, followers and connections. I will conclude this chapter with an overview of Blogging.

The easy bit is to set up your company page. The difficult part is to get people to engage with you, your content or your followers. To get them to like you, follow you, comment on your posts or share your posts.

Facebook is the biggest when it comes to engagement. On average, Facebook users spent more than 400 minutes per month on Facebook. People also spend a lot of time on Pinterest. LinkedIn, Google+ and Twitter are lagging behind. Although you could say that the time people spend on Facebook is in short intervals. The younger generation uses Facebook in bursts. They get their smart phone out of their pocket, send somebody a Facebook message and that's it. 10 minutes later they make a photo of what they are eating and they share it on their Facebook newsfeed. For brands, this style of interaction doesn't allow for giving their fans a more in depth brand experience. Maybe that is the secret of Google+ for brands. Sessions on Google+ tend to be longer. Which gives brands more opportunity to develop brand engagement with their followers.

Facebook

Facebook is a social network that has core Social Media functionality and a number of apps to enrich the user experience. The main features are the Homepage or the Profile and the Newsfeed where you can see all the engagement activity from your friends.

To get started on Facebook you sign up, you create your personal Profile, you connect with Friends and then you start engaging.

Businesses are not allowed to use a person's personal Profile to promote their business. They have to create a Company Page. By creating a Company Page you can get people to like your page by pressing the like button. From then on they may see the updates from your company in their personal news feed. The better your content you share on your page, the more likely people will see it.

Here are the most popular features that are being used by Facebook members. So take this into consideration when you plan your engagement strategy.

Number 10: Facebook Events. Facebook Events is a really good way to drive engagement on Facebook. You announce your event and then you engage with your audience before, during and after the event. Facebook has upgraded its Events feature. You can now brand your Facebook Events Page and build engagement around your events.

Number 9: Facebook Timeline. Facebook Timeline was announced last year. It is a chronological order by month and by year of your Posts on your profile page. It changed the concept of Facebook drastically. From Facebook being a "now" social network, it became a "yesterday, now and tomorrow" social network. It gives people the opportunity to create a scrapbook of their lives. Your live becomes a visual presentation of yourself, your Friends or whatever topic you love. There was a lot of discussion when Facebook announced. People didn't want their friends to see their posts from the past. But nowadays, everybody got used to it. Facebook allowed people to clean up their Facebook Timeline. For businesses, the Timeline is a great way to engage with their fans. Fans can now collect all the memorabilia of the brands they adore. Of course, only when the brand has populated its timeline. And fans cannot only collect, they can also engage on the content, with the brand and with other fans. This is a whole new way of engagement.

Number 8: Social Plugins. Social Plugins allow you to comment on your Facebook wall from outside Facebook. It brings Facebook functionality outside Facebook. It has significantly widened the footprint of Facebook. Millions of websites are now integrated with Facebook through social plugins.

Number 7: Embed in Post. This enables you to embed a link to a web page in your post. It will also pick up the graphics associate with that page. So you can visualise the content that you are sharing.

Number 6: The Wall. The Wall is your personal home page on Facebook. It is the page where you can see everything that you've shared on Facebook. This is a very handy feature to find out what content people have shared and what has happened with it in terms of likes and comments.

Number 5: Relationship Status. With this feature people can say, "I'm in a relationship", "I'm not in a relationship", "It is complicated". It is a feature that the younger generation loves to use.

Feature 4: Facebook Messenger. This is a very powerful feature and many Facebook users use this as an alternative to email. Their primary channel of communication with their friends is Facebook Messenger. It works particularly well on mobile. Remember the big messaging networks? MSN, Yahoo Chat? What has happened to them? Microsoft has announced that they will close down MSN. Messaging has now moved to the (mobile) social networks.

Number 3: The Like button. I Like your Post. I like your company Page. As soon as you like a company Page, you will see the updates of that company in your own News feed. It is a masterstroke of Facebook – a very powerful and a very simple way to drive engagement on your Facebook Page or your personal Facebook site.

Number 2: The Newsfeed. The Newsfeed brings together all the Facebook activities of your friends. Facebook came out with this a number of years ago and nowadays all social networks have adopted this concept. It is the main driver for engagement where you see in one glance what all the people in your network are doing.

Number 1: Photo Sharing. Facebook is all about sharing emotions, sharing how you feel, sharing what you do. There's no better way of showing this to your friends then through a photo. If you see somebody making a photo in a restaurant of the meal they are eating, most likely, the photo will be posted on Facebook straightaway. It is the most popular feature on Facebook, and literally millions and millions of Photos are being uploaded, shared, liked and commented on everyday.

Facebook's 3 pillar strategy

Facebook has done a number of major announcements over the last 18 months. They completed the three pillars of Facebook's strategy:

1.   Facebook Timeline
2.   Facebook Graph Search
3.   Facebook Newsfeed

Facebook Timeline. A very powerful feature which gave a new dimension to the Facebook experience. It is a new way of engaging. It is no longer about what is happening today, but it allows you to build your personal or your company's scrapbook, photo book, diary of your life or your company's history.

Facebook Graph Search. Search is slowly moving away from the traditional search engines like Google and Bing. It is moving into the social networks. When you search in your social network, you get the search results from your Friends. If I search in Twitter, I can search what my Twitter Followers are saying or I can search the whole Twitter community. If I search on LinkedIn, I can search what my connections are saying in LinkedIn. Facebook Graph Search allows you to search in your own Facebook world. You can search who of your Friends like skiing in the French Alps or what their favorite restaurant is in London.

Facebook Newsfeed. Facebook recently announced an upgrade to the Newsfeed, making it visually more attractive and making it more engaging. A bigger focus on the visualisation. The timeline now also include hashtags. People can see other people's content that is related to the subject of the post.

Facebook for Business

So how can a business benefit from Facebook? Companies have 4 tools available to promote their business:
1.   Facebook Groups
2.   Facebook Pages
3.   Facebook Apps
4.   Facebook Advertising

Facebook Groups

Facebook Groups reside in the personal world of people's Facebook. You can create a Group and within that Group, you can connect with other Facebook users. A retail brand for example can have a Facebook Group to manage the working schedules for their staff of each store. Employees can manage and exchange their shifts in the Facebook Group. All group members will see updates in their newsfeed when somebody offers his/her shift to the group. This will save the company a lot of time in staff planning.

Facebook Page

The main way to promote your business is through a Facebook Page. Facebook does not allow you to use your personal Facebook account to promote your business. You create an admin account as a personal user but you are not going to use this as a personal account. You use that account to create your Facebook Page.

You should brand your Facebook Page in line with your corporate brand and then you start growing your following by getting people to like your Facebook Page. When somebody likes your Facebook Page they will see all your company updates on their personal newsfeed. They can like or comment on your company posts, which will then expose your content to their friends. This makes facebook so powerful for businesses. If you have good content, it can spread like wildfire on Facebook.

The key components of your Facebook Page are:

- **Cover Photo,** Your place for branding your page.
- **Profile Picture.** Most companies use their logo.
- **Timeline.** You populate your timeline as far back as you want. For brands this is a new and innovative way of engaging with their fans.
- **Messaging area.** You can send messages to your fans.
- **About section.** The place where you can give more details about your business.
- **Facebook Apps.** A maximum of 12 Apps that you can add to drive engagement. Only four Apps are visible "above the fold". The first app is always your Photos. The other apps can be in any order.
- **Pin Posts.** You can pin posts to the top for seven days. This is good for promoting specific posts.
- **Photos in your posts.** Photos can be a normal-sized photo spanning one side of the timeline or it can be a Milestone photo spanning both sides.

The best Facebook Pages are about fun, people and emotion. They are about people sharing what they love. Coca-Cola is the most liked Facebook Page. They have no problem in getting 60+ million likes because there are many brand aficionados out there who love to find out everything they can about Coca-Cola. And even better, they can now engage with Coca Cola and with other fans. Something that can never be done on the Coca Cola web site.

The Rolling Stones don't have a problem in getting 12 million likes because their fans are passionate about the music and the band. In general, we say that Facebook Pages are good for consumer brands and the more passion there is around the consumer brand, the easier it will be to create a big following on the brand's Facebook Page.

Facebook Pages is not only for consumer brands. There are B2B (Business to Business) companies that use Facebook very effectively. Big companies with many employees can create a Facebook Page to showcase the company's world to their employees and thereby showcasing it to their family. It gives everybody the feel-good factor about working for the company. Many companies also use their Facebook page for recruitment, to target a younger audience.

Growing your following

When you have your Facebook page ready, the next challenge is to increase your following by getting people to like your Facebook page. The more people like your Facebook page, the more people will see your Posts. There are various ways to increase your following on facebook.

- First of all, promote your Facebook Page. Promote it offline and promote it online. Put "Like us on Facebook" in your shop, on your company van, on you business card and in your catalogue. Put it on your website. Put it in your e-mail signature. Tell the world that you are on Facebook.

- Suggest it to friends. Ask friends to like your page. Send your customers an e-mail and ask them to like your Facebook page. Reward them with a freebee.

- Use the Share button. If you want your content to be seen more often by your friends and fans you need to use the Share button. The Share button has a higher authority within Facebook than the Like button.

- Use Events. Events are great to drive engagement on your Facebook Page. They go to a wider audience on Facebook and you can engage with your attendees before, during and after the event.

Facebook Apps

The best way to grow your following is to run campaigns or promotions through Facebook Apps. You can have a maximum of 12 Apps per Page. You can change the order of the Apps, but you can't change the first one. The first App is always the Photos app. You can change the Icons and more importantly, you can create your own Facebook App. You can ask your agency to create an App. You can also go to sites like shortstack.com where you can create your own App for free.

Apps give you the opportunity to integrate deeply with the Facebook experience. You can create an app as a landing page that promotes your campaign, or as a page to promote your like button. We call this a fan-gate. Fan-gating (also known as "Like-gating") is the concept of getting more fans for you Facebook page by asking Facebook users to "like" your page in order to access specific content. This content is typically exclusive features, promotional offers, games or other material. This is a really good way to drive engagement and get people to like your Facebook page.

There are other ways to drive engagement. Use large post images. It is important to make your Facebook timeline very visual. Visitors must see and feel that it is an engaging experience. Highlight posts through Milestones. You can do link-to-Apps from your website. You can run a contest or an exclusive offer, or promote exclusive content. These are important ways to get that extra engagement going.

Here are some other tips to drive engagement on your Facebook page.

- **Give your Page the human touch.** People do business with people. Companies do business with people so show the people behind your brand. Show the people behind the Facebook Page. Showcase your business from a "people" perspective. Don't talk anonymously. Talk about you as a person, and about your clients or your followers as a person. It is very important to give your Page that human touch.

- **Make sure that you have diversity in your content.** It is not just text. There should be photos, videos, polls and infographics. There are lots of different types of content to get people to engage with your brand.

- **Make sure that your dialogue is two-way.** Everything you do on your Facebook is about asking for engagement. You can post a photo with "This is us on a Friday afternoon." But to get this two-way dialogue, it should be "This is us on a Friday afternoon. What is your Friday afternoon like?" Ask questions. Get into a dialogue.

- **Get calls to action in your Facebook page posts.** People need to click to get something or achieve something. Click here to download, click here to register, click here to participate or go to the website to do this. In doing this you have an opportunity to get their contact details.

- **Run campaigns that facilitate word-of-mouth advocacy.** Try to you get people to talk about your Facebook page or your Facebook campaign. People get curious and will check out your page. There are some really good examples of people starting to talk about a Facebook campaign. One of the most famous and controversial Facebook campaigns was the Whopper Sacrifice from Burger King. They wanted to challenge Facebook's concept of friends. Saying that many people have friends on Facebook that are not really friends. So they put this to the test by offering people a free whopper voucher for every 10 friends they deleted. Many people started deleting their friends on Facebook. Facebook stepped in and changed the functionality of the site so the campaign would no longer work. Burger King had to sacrifice the whopper sacrifice and withdrew the campaign. But it generated huge brand exposure for them and it is still being referred to as one of the best campaigns ever on Facebook.

- **Encouraging conversation between your fans** is another important way to drive engagement. Get your fans to communicate with each other. Get fans to upload content and let other fans evaluate that content. In doing so you encourage conversation and engagement.

- **Brand your Facebook smartly.** There are some really good examples like Coca-Cola or Starbucks. They use clever branding in design and messaging. Facebook has eased the restrictions on the cover photo. It can't have more than 20% text but it can now have promotions, calls to action and even an arrow to the like button.

Global Facebook Pages

Facebook also give you the opportunity to create Global Pages. Global brands with a Facebook presence in multiple countries can now create a network of pages. You will get the page from the country that you are in. If there is no Facebook page for that country, you will be referred to the Global Page. All likes are aggregated on the global page and are also shown on each local page. You can run your own Facebook campaign with local content targeting local people. You can localise your Cover Photo, your Profile Photo, the Apps, your Mailbox, the URL, the Milestones, the About section. You also get local Facebook insights data.

You can also publish targeted Posts in Facebook. You can target by gender, relationship status, education, interested in, location and language. You can zoom in on particular areas and particular interests with your Posts. It increases the relevance of your Post, giving you higher response rate, longer fan retention, greater control, more personalisation of your content, improved optimisation and prolonged visibility so more people will see your content that's relevant to them.

Facebook Advertising

A very important feature on Facebook for businesses is Facebook Advertising. It is designed to help you show people adverts they find interesting and relevant. The ads they see are selected based on the things they do on Facebook, such as liking a Page or commenting on a story, and the information they share, such as current city or birthday. Ads can also be selected based on information that people share.

Facebook has different type of ads:

Page Like Ad - the standard Facebook Ad. This is the standard form of a Facebook ad and appears on the right-hand side of the screen and on user's newsfeed, and directs you on a specified Facebook page.

Sponsored Stories - This type of ad is generated from fans' interactions with your Facebook page. It gives an overview of a fan's recent action with your page, such as a like or comment, and then shows it as an ad to his/her friends.

Page Post or Promoted Post Ad - A Page Post Ad lets you use a recent post/action on your Facebook page as an ad. So if you've just added something like a video, text, event, link, or a question to your Facebook page, you can promote it and show it to your fans.

Mobile App Install Ads – These ads drive mobile app downloads and send users directly to an app download page, rather than prompt users for likes. These ads are usually in a separate module, like a Sponsored Story, and appear on the newsfeed in the mobile version.

The Domain Facebook Ad – The Domain Facebook Ad or External Website Ad, appears on the right-hand side of the screen only and directs you away from Facebook to an external website.

Twitter

Twitter is SMS on steroids. The basic concept is very simple. You follow people on Twitter. Those people send tweets. These are 140-character messages. You will receive the tweets of the people that you follow. So if you follow a lot of people, you will get a lot of tweets. Then people follow you. Your followers will receive the tweets you send. You will receive Tweets from people that you follow; the people that follow you will receive your tweets. With the millions of Twitter users across the world, there's a whole world of tweets going back and forth on the web.

It is straightforward to follow people. You search for people you want to follow on Twitter and when you find them you click follow. It is more difficult to get people to follow you because then you need to add value. They need to have a reason to follow you.

What makes Twitter so viral?

First of all, I can retweet a tweet I receive. when I retweet a tweet, my followers will receive that tweet. A tweet sent by one person can trickle down and can be global across the world in a very short time. That's what happened when Andy Murray won Wimbledon. He tweeted saying, "I can't believe what is happening to me," and millions of people started to retweet that. This went across the web in no time.

2.   The second reason why Twitter is so viral is that you can add a link to a photo, a video or a website to your tweet. You can direct people to other places on the web. Twitter now becomes a search engine for good content.

3.   The third reason why Twitter is so viral is

because of the Hashtag.   The # symbol, called a hashtag, is used to mark keywords or topics in a Tweet. It was created organically by Twitter users as a way to categorize messages. People use the hashtag symbol before a relevant keyword or phrase in their Tweet to categorise those Tweets and help them show more easily in Twitter Search. Clicking on a hashtagged word in any message shows you all other Tweets marked with that keyword. Hashtagged words that become very popular are often Trending Topics.

The Hashtag for the London Olympics was #London2012. If you wanted to stay up-to-date with what was happening during the London Olympics, you could search for #London2012 and you got all the relevant Tweets. And by adding this hashtag to your own tweets you can participate in the discussion.

There are two ways of Tweeting. There is the celebrity Tweeting. For fans, it is a fantastic way to engage and to stay up-to-date with what the celebrity is doing. For businesses, it is different. Businesses use Twitter to share content to keep in touch with your customers. Some business people think they are a celebrity. They start tweeting about last night's party or the movie they are about to see. Personally, I don't use Twitter like this. I am not interested in the personal whereabouts of my business contacts. And I don't think anybody is interested in mine.

So, how do you get started on Twitter? You sign up and set up your Twitter Profile. Then you start searching on Twitter for people to follow. This is the easy bit. Getting people to follow you is more difficult. Then you start to listen, share and engage on Twitter. It is all about driving engagement, finding content and finding leads. It is about building relationships with your most important influencers on Twitter.

Your Twitter homepage

Your Twitter Homepage has your Twitter profile, also known as your Twitter bio. Many people ignore their Bio. Your home page is your opportunity to showcase your brand and your key messages. When people go on Twitter and check you out, they click on your bio. When you write you bio think about your target audience. Why would they be interested in you? You can also brand the background that you use on your Twitter page and the background that you use behind your bio. People put key messages, key contact data or their presence on other social networks on their Twitter background.

Following people on Twitter

Once your bio is ready, you then have to find people to follow. How do you find people on Twitter? You can use the Twitter Search or you can use other search engines. You can also use Twitter Directories which can be seen as the Yellow Pages of Twitter users.

Twitter's Advanced Search is a very powerful feature. You not only search for words, but you can also search for people. Once you connect with somebody on Twitter, Twitter will tell you if you know this person, you might want to follow this person as well. If you see somebody you want to follow, then check the followers of that person because they might be interesting people for you to follow as well. In your Listening stage you identified your top bloggers. Start following them as well. And start following other thought leaders you know.

Events are really good to get to know people on Twitter Start collecting Twitter names at events. If the event has a

Hashtag, listen in during the events and start following those people.

One of my favorites is Followerwonk.com which allows you to search in Twitter bios. The search results will give you also a reputation score of the twitter profiles you find.

Getting people to follow you on Twitter

Getting people to follow you is a bit more difficult. There needs to be a value for people to follow you so you need to create a reason for people to follow you. You need to find out what they need. Why would they want to follow you? What kind of content would they need from you? What kind of links would you share? What do they talk about? Try to understand who your audience is and then address their needs.

Some guidelines in getting people to follow you on Twitter:

- Make sure your Twitter name is easy to find and it is related to your company. Sometimes that can be difficult if you have a common name.

- Place Follow buttons on your website, on your blog, on your e-mail signature. Tell the world that you are on Twitter. Use that little bird logo and put it everywhere.

- Interact with the people you follow, but don't follow you back.

- Make your tweets useful.

Here are some more tips to build your following:

- Pay attention to your Profile.
- Retweet other people's content but don't retweet yourself to the top.
- Use Twitter Directories.
- Use Hashtags.
- Go to Tweetups where people chat live on Twitter.
- Participate in those Tweetups.
- Tweet during events.

When you have a base of followers, you are going to start tweeting and here are some suggestions of what you can tweet about:

- You can tweet about something you see. If you are in architecture and you see a really nice building that is very well designed, then why not make a photo of it and tweet about it?
- Tweet what you are reading. If it is an interesting book or an interesting article, tweet about this.
- Tweet something that you are watching.
- Tweet about events that you are attending.
- Tweet your own content.
- Tweet somebody else's content.
- Retweet what somebody else has tweeted.

There was a documentary about Facebook on TV the other day. While I was watching it, I tweeted to my followers, saying; "If you are watching TV – very interesting Facebook documentary." The next day, I tweeted it again. But then with the link to BBC iPlayer.

You can also communicate directly with people on twitter. You can send a message to people you are not connected with by including @username in your tweet. Or you can send a direct message to people who you follow and follow you back. A great way to re-connect with people you know but you lost their email.

Finding leads on Twitter

A powerful aspect of Twitter is to search for leads. How do you find leads on Twitter? To do this successfully you have to define appropriate streams with the right keywords in your listening station. People are looking for your product or service, request information to solve problems, complain about competition or participate in relevant discussions. You need to understand the profile of the people that are looking for your products and services, and what they are looking for.

Searching for leads starts with searching for questions. You can search for "CRM software" and you get all the Tweets that include CRM software. But when you search for "CRM software?" you are getting Tweets from people who ask questions with the word "CRM software". Questions like "Can anybody give me advice on what CRM software I should buy?"

You can search for people in Twitter. If you are going to meet somebody, you can search for that person and identify what they have tweeted about. This will help you to open the conversation when you meet face to face.

Twitter recently announced Twitter Lead Generation Cards. You can put a call to action in your tweets. People can click to get a screen where they need to fill in their contact details or their e-mail details.

To organize your Followers you can use Twitter Lists. You can join lists, you can create your own lists, or you can scan lists or import them into your listening station to listen to specific lists of people.

Finally

Don't automate. You can use tools that will automatically send out your tweets according a set schedule. They can randomly pick your tweets from a database. But as soon as people get the slightest incline that you are not tweeting yourself, they will switch off. Don't promote yourself relentlessly. It is about engagement. Don't stalk or abuse people. People might complain to you and you can respond to that, but as soon as it gets nasty, take the discussion offline, away from your Twitter.

LinkedIn

LinkedIn can help you reach your business goals and it can help you reach the mutual contacts who can introduce you to the people that you want to meet. The power of LinkedIn is in the second degree. They are the connections of your connections. Through your connections you can access their connections and expand your network.

I call LinkedIn "Facebook with a tie". In LinkedIn, you want to be visible and professional. In Facebook, you are worried about your privacy settings. In LinkedIn, you actually want people to know as much as possible because it is the business card of your career. It is your CV, but it is a lot more than that. It is the world's largest professional network on the Internet with more than 200 million members in over 200 countries.

On linkedIn Members create their professional identity online and engage with their professional network to develop their online reputation. They can access and share knowledge and insights, and find business opportunities. It is the most extensive, accurate and accessible network focused on professionals. It is the most business like network of all Social Media networks and it is growing very fast with two people signing up every second. LinkedIn's mission is to connect the world's professionals to make them more productive and successful.

The three pillars of LinkedIn

The first pillar: Talent Management. LinkedIn has reinvented recruitment. In LinkedIn, you can find jobs or you can promote your jobs as a business. When a business has a job opening, they can upload the job description on

LinkedIn. LinkedIn will give them a listing of the LinkedIn profiles with the closest match. They can then proactively approach those people in LinkedIn. Talent Management is a key pillar and a key revenue generator.

The second pillar: Media space. LinkedIn offers media space for companies to advertise. It works exactly like Facebook advertising. You can target specific audiences and payment, you can set an advertising budget and you can pay for the ads by credit card. Larger companies can have big advertising contracts on LinkedIn to reach the global business community.

The third pillar: Sales. You can use LinkedIn to be more effective in selling. It's an incredibly powerful tool for sales people. Sales people can use LinkedIn to:
- Connect with customers and prospects.
- Use the extensive LinkedIn Search, engagement and Group tools to find people and analyse companies.
- Build relationships with people.
- Develop themselves as an expert.

You can have a standard account on LinkedIn, or you can have a Premium Account. A Premium Account will give you many additional features. The most popular ones are:
- InMail to send e-mails within LinkedIn to people that you are not connected with.
- A Profile Organizer to organise the Profiles of the people in your network.
- Additional search filters.
- More profile results per search.
- Save more search alerts.

These are good reasons to upgrade your account.

Particularly when you are a LinkedIn power user.

How to get started on LinkedIn?

You sign up for LinkedIn; you personalise your LinkedIn Profile; you grow your network; you join Groups; and you engage with your network. As a business, you create your company Page and get people to connect with your company Page so they will see your company updates on their personal news feed.

Most people in LinkedIn sign up, personalise their profile, grow their network and join Groups. But then they stop. They don't engage. That's LinkedIn's biggest challenge. All interface and functionality changes LinkedIn made in the last year are geared towards getting more people to engage by sharing good content and participating in discussions.

Your LinkedIn Profile

Your LinkedIn profile is key. Your LinkedIn Profile is YOUR Profile. It is not your company's Profile. Your LinkedIn Profile should be written in a way that you don't have to rewrite your LinkedIn profile if you join another company.

Why is your personal Profile so important? People will check you out. People will search for you on Google and they will search for you on LinkedIn. If they have a meeting with you or if you are applying for a job, they will check you out on LinkedIn. If you say one thing on LinkedIn and they find something completely different in Google, that may work against you. LinkedIn is your online showcase and the better your profile, the higher you will come up in the search results. Not only in LinkedIn but also in Google. Search for yourself in Google and see what comes up. Are you happy with what you see? Does it confirm your online reputation from a professional perspective? Now do the same search on LinkedIn. Is it consistent with what people will see in Google? The quality of your LinkedIn Profile influences what people will see and read about you online. It confirms your expertise. People might become interested in talking to you. More and more people will look for you on LinkedIn and Google before they have a meeting with you.

There are five elements in your LinkedIn Profile.

1. Your teaser, your one-liner about what makes you different.
2. Your picture and name, professional headline, location and industry.
3. A short background or summary.
4. Your specialties, your experience, your education.
5. The details. Like your awards, hobbies, projects, recommendations etc.

LinkedIn will give you a percentage completeness. Aim for "all stars" and if you are not there yet, LinkedIn will give you recommendations with links to what you need to do next.

Under your name, don't say, "Marketing Manager for Company (A-B-C)", but give it your personal elevator pitch. "Marketing Manager specialized in…" or "Innovative Sales Director focusing on…" Have your personal keywords and uses these. LinkedIn and Google like keywords. Make your summary crisp and clear.

There are lots of ways to improve your LinkedIn Profile. Use video in your background info or in your jobs. Use Recommendations. Use projects. Never lie on your LinkedIn Profile. It goes without saying. Never misrepresent your employment history on your Profile. One day, it will come back to you.

Also work on your LinkedIn Skills section. Add a list of your skills and then people can endorse you for those skills. That is very important. It might seem irrelevant but when used properly it will be your personal tag cloud where people, in one glance, can see what you are all about.

Growing your connections

When your profile is ready, and you've added your skills and some recommendations you have to grow your connections. There are multiple degrees of Connections in LinkedIn:

1. **First-degree Connections** are people that you are directly connected with because you have accepted their invitation to connect or they have accepted your invitation. In LinkedIn, you can contact them by sending them a message. That's the easiest way to contact people once you are a first-degree Connection.
2. **Second-degree Connections** are the people who are connected to your first-degree Connections. You can connect with them by sending them an invite to connect. A better way is to see if you have a shared Connection and you ask the shared Connection to give you an introduction. You can only contact second-degree Connections through an InMail.
3. **Third-degree Connections** are people that are

connected to your second-degree Connections. They are considered to be in your network. If you only see the first letter of their last name, then you can't connect with them, but then you can still send them an InMail.

4. **Fellow members of LinkedIn Groups.** They are not connected to you, but they are considered part of your network because you are members of the same Group. Interestingly, you can send these people a message within the Group. That's one of the secrets within LinkedIn. So if you find a third-degree Connection that you really want to connect with without having to upgrade to a Premium Account, check what Group he or she is a member of, join that Group and then engage in a conversation within the LinkedIn Group.

How do you expand your Connections? First step is to upload your e-mail contacts and connect with the ones already on LinkedIn. Step two – find current and former colleagues and classmates. You can search for the company or search for the university. Step three – LinkedIn will give you, "If you know this person, you also might know these people", once you've connected with somebody. It is important to promote your LinkedIn Profile on your e-mail, on your website and in your blog.

When you want to connect with somebody, you can click the connect button and that person will automatically get a request to connect from you. In some cases you will get a pop-up screen in which you have to specify how you know that person.

LinkedIn Search

A very powerful feature in LinkedIn is LinkedIn Search. You can search for people, companies and groups. You can also search for news.

There are multiple ways to find people in the advanced search section of LinkedIn:

1. You can search for the name of that person.
2. You can search for different parameters. For example, you can search for "Marketing Director at Shell in Scotland" for example.
3. You can browse in the network of your network.
4. Look at the Connections of your connections.
5. Look at, "Viewers of this Profile also viewed viewers of that Profile".
6. Check members of your groups
7. Check out the Groups that your Contacts have joined. In those Groups you may find interesting people for you to connect with.
8. Find people by checking the company pages.

In the free LinkedIn account you can save up to three searches. You can save more searches in the premium account.

Here's a point of caution. Be careful with accepting invitations of people you don't know. Try to keep your LinkedIn network as genuine, as clean as possible. I only connect with people on LinkedIn that I know or where I have clear business interest to know these people.

If you find a third-level Connection with first name and first letter last name, then you won't know who that person is. What you can then do is search for that person in Google. So put "Jane C" and the company name in Google, and then often, Google will come back to you with the full LinkedIn name of that person and a link to their public profile.

There are lots of benefits in looking at Profiles of prospects. You find additional connections, but very important, you will show up as a visitor on that person's Profile. So you position yourself as somebody that has shown an interest in that person.

You can also search for companies. When you search for companies, you can see if you have people in your network working for that company or you can get access to a list of people working for that company.

LinkedIn Groups

LinkedIn Groups are really good for listening, engaging and developing your own reputation. You can join Groups that are relevant to your business or you can create your own Group. Groups can be public, closed or private. Private groups will not show in search results. Companies use private LinkedIn Groups to communicate internally.

Post your blogs and articles in your Groups so that you get the attention of other Group members. Engage with people seeking help that your business can solve. Use Groups to listen for opportunities and engage with other group members.

Before you join a Group, always check the LinkedIn Groups analytics. Check the demographics, the growth and the activity levels in the Group. If the Group is very small or there is little activity, the LinkedIn Group analytics will give you that info and it might not be worthwhile joining that Group.

LinkedIn Pulse

LinkedIn Pulse is the news service in LinkedIn. It is the place to share and engage on news and interesting content. The LinkedIn Pulse that you will see on your LinkedIn homepage will be different than the LinkedIn Pulse of somebody else. The news you see is based on your Profile. You can select specific channels on different news topics. LinkedIn Pulse has also asked global and industry thought leaders to write for LinkedIn Pulse to enhance its value and reputation.

LinkedIn Company page

To promote your company on LinkedIn, you create your company Page. It works exactly the same as the Facebook Page. You get people to connect with your company Page and then people will see your company updates on their personal news feed.

As a small business or just as an individual with your own business, you don't necessarily need to engage on your LinkedIn company page. But my advice is to get a company page anyway. In your Profile you can link to your company Page and it will show up as a promotional business card when people hover over your company name. If you don't have that, LinkedIn will show, "Click here to find other people that work for this company". That's a lost branding opportunity.

The elements of your company Page are the company Homepage, the Careers section, the Products & Services section and the Insights. On the Homepage you have a banner that you can use to promote your business. You can have a Career section where you can promote your business and the jobs you have on offer. This is a premium feature. On the Products section, you can create different Product sections with multiple tabs, and people can endorse or Recommend your products as well. It is not as powerful in branding as a Facebook Page, but more and more features will be coming into this. You can add video to the different Product sections as well. Insights will give you very good analytics about traffic and engagement on your company page.

LinkedIn recently announced Showcase Pages. They allow you to create different product pages for different people, depending on their profile characteristics. For example, a marketing manager could see a different product page than a purchasing manager.

Google+

Google positions Google+ as the new Google. It is Google's social layer over all their products, and they will bring more and more products into Google+ over time. If you want to take advantage of all the Google features, then you have to use Google+. One day, you will end up using Google+. It also helps you in your search rankings because it is part of Google. More and more people are getting this message, and more and more people are getting onto Google+.

Google+ has now over 400 million active users. It is the second-biggest social network and billions of items are being shared everyday. One of the key engagement drivers on Google+ is Google Hangouts. This is video conferencing that you can stream live on Youtube.

Here are the key features in Google+

- News Stream
- Your Profile
- Google Circles
- Photo sharing
- What is Hot
- Communities
- Events
- Google Hangouts
- Company Page
- Local Page

Google News Stream

Google News Stream, your newsfeed, is very easy to use. You can adjust the number of columns so it fits multiple devices. You have video and photos that you can stretch to multiple columns and you can dive deeper in posts via Hashtags. There are cool animated effects to make the newsfeed more exciting. You can see post activity and it is very easy to format text in your Posts.

Google Circles

A key feature in Google+ is Google Circles. Contrary to Facebook where everybody is your friend, Google+ allows you to group your friends in circles. You can send your post to the relevant circles. You can create your own circles. It is a great way to segment your following. You can also search for people in circles. When you create a post, you can select which Circle you want to send it to. It is a very powerful feature and one of the key differentiators of Google+, particularly from a business point of view. You can also join public Circles which is a great way of finding new people to connect with.

There are lots of advantages of using Google Circles:
- You can create distinct groups of people in your social network so you can share specific information with only those people rather than your whole network.
- You can look at updates from your business contacts. You can select specific Circles that you want the updates from.
- People you don't know can follow you, but you don't need to add them back to your Circles.
- People who follow you will only see updates and information that you have shared publicly, similar to Twitter, but unlike Facebook. To get people to see your content, they need to be in your circles and you need to be in their circles.

When you share a Post or update, Google+ automatically defaults to the last Circle it was shared with so you need to check this before publishing new updates.

What's Hot?

Google+ What's Hot feature is similar to what is Trending on Twitter. There is a specific What's Hot newsfeed and you can define if there are specific What's Hot elements you want to have featured on your own newsfeed.

Google+ Search

Search in Google+ is one of the main advantages. You can Search by post, circles, groups, community, event or by page. Obviously, this is where Google brings in its experience in Search. You can Search for exactly the type of content that you want.

Google Communities

In Google Communities you can create Communities around your company or your product. You can Search within communities as well. It is good to create awareness about your brand. Particularly when you start your own Community. You maintain authority around your topics. They are indexed by Google Search and it is a really good place to engage with active users in Google+.

Google Events

Google Events is very powerful. You can add a Google Hangout to a public Event. This allows you to promote your event live on Youtube or broadcast a virtual event. You can also add Party mode which allows people attending the event to upload their photos real-time during the Event. Google Events is integrated with Google Calendar and email and has excellent event analytics.

Google Hangouts

Google Hangouts is video conferencing and broadcasting. This can be peer to peer, with maximum 9 people. It has the option to stream your Hangout live on Youtube. When President Obama was re-elected as President, he did a Google Hangout with nine top journalists the following day where they could ask him questions. It was streamed live on Youtube for millions of people to watch.

Google hangouts has lots of applications for businesses. It is great for crowd sourcing to get the community to suggest ideas on how your product or your service can be improved. It is good for questions and answers sessions with your customers. You can demonstrate a product, run webinars or pull back the curtain to show what happening behind the scenes in your company.

Google+ Company page

As a business you create your Google+ Page. It is the same concept as Facebook Pages and LinkedIn Pages. You need to get people to Connect with your company Page and then they will see your updates in their news feed. You can create a page for a product or a brand, a company, institution, organisation, a local business place, arts and entertainment, sports or other.

If you are a local business you must consider integrating your local Page with your company Page. If you do that, people can review your business and add a star rating. You can also add a link to Google Maps on your Google+ page. You need to do a Page verification to combine the two.

So the key question, "Should you go on Google+?" If you've got good content, if you've got good visuals and if you want to be seen as an innovative company – yes, you want to be an early adopter. If segmentation is important for you, then you definitely have to be on Google+. One day, you will end up using it.

Pinterest

Pinterest is a virtual pinboard that allows users to organize and share beautiful and interesting content they find on the web. If you see an interesting photo you can click a button in your browser called Pin It and that button will connect the link with your pinboard. You are not downloading the photo, but you are bookmarking it. You are showcasing that photo on your pinboard. When people click on that photo in the pinboard, it will direct them to the source web page of that photo. It is really good to drive traffic to specific places on the web. It is visually very powerful.

Pinterest's goal is to connect everyone in the world through the things they find interesting. If you are interested in recipes, you can find pinboards on recipes. If you are interested in outdoor, you can find pinboards on outdoor. So if you know your target audience, and know what they are interested in, you can create pinboards with beautiful content in relation to these topics. You can promote your Pinterest Page on your web site and your social media sites.

IKEA UK has a Pinterest Page with pinboards on bedrooms, kitchens, living rooms etc. When you go on a board and you click a photo, you will be directed to the company's online catalogue. Where you can buy the product you liked.

Pinterest has many benefits for your business:

- It has great potential for retailers;
- It can help you boost your brand image by sharing cool, relevant images;
- It is good to digitise your catalogue and to drive

    traffic to your catalogue;
- People get inspired and will share your content on Pinterest. That generates a viral effect;
- It will generate leads;
- It drives traffic to your website;

Pinterest is a very powerful tool for business when you have great and inspiring content to share.

Instagram

Instagram is a fun and quirky way to share your life with friends through a series of pictures. You can snap a photo with your mobile phone, then choose a filter to transform the photo into your own piece of photo art. Instagram allows you to experience moments in your friends' lives through pictures as they happen.

All photos are public by default which means they are visible to anyone using Instagram or on the instagram.com website. By adding hashtags to their photos people can easily search for photos on Instagram. If you choose to make your account private, then only people who follow you on Instagram will be able to see your photos.

Instagram for business

Use Instagram to post images of your brand, products and services that allow your customers to enter deeper into your world. Or even better, allow them to share their own stories (through imagery) and make them feel a part of your world.

Post pictures during events or product launches, provide sneak peeks or behind the scenes exclusive footage to allow your followers to get a glimpse of your exclusive brand world. Bring your customers into your space by using pictures to tell your story.

Like Twitter, people assign hashtags to certain pictures, places, products and services. So make sure you know what hashtags people are using when they talk about your brand.

Hashtags are a really great way to find people who are talking about your brand and to follow their photos and conversations. As a brand you can also start using certain hashtags when talking about your products, services or elements of your business – another way to extend the reach of your brand stories.

Instagram took Facebook's photo-sharing, Twitter's hashtags and Foursquare's location tags and meshed them all into one. Any great story has a great location and Instagram's geo-tags allow you to share yours.

Instagram's geo-tagging feature can help link specific campaigns to certain locations, and allow people to post, view and share images linked to these locations. Geo-tagging is a great way to advertise your brand's presence at a particular conference or event as well as a valuable way to market an event that you plan on hosting. With the recent upgrades, geo-tags are also able to transfer location information to Facebook, Flickr, Foursquare or Twitter.

Youtube

Youtube is the world's biggest video-sharing community and it is considered the second-biggest search engine in the world. The numbers are impressive. Over one hour of video uploaded on Youtube every second. Youtube is only eight years old and in those eight years, they have grown to support incredible volumes of video that are now being made available online. Billions of hours of video are watched each month. 39 countries, 54 languages, trillions of views.

Bands are being created overnight on Youtube. Justin Bieber started on Youtube. It is the lingua franca of the business world. Youtube has made online video accessible to every corner of the world. A large part of Youtube's success is driven by mobile video.

Video drives Social Media engagement because it is the type of content that touches the emotions of people. An image says a thousand words; a video says a million words. When you can see what is being said and when you combine seeing with what you are hearing, then the retention is much, much higher.

Why is it so powerful? It is because it is the most powerful on-demand communication platform ever created. It is visual and you decide when and where you want to watch it. It is highly viral. People who love to watch videos, share them on their social networks and promote them on their blog or website. It is very high-impact and it scales very well on a mobile phone.

Video can play an important role for companies. It helps them to:

- Develop brand awareness;
- Advertise products;
- Promote products;
- Sell more effectively;
- Support products through video;
- Train customers via Youtube;
- Communicate internally;
- Use it as a recruitment channel.

Video has become available on a low budget. You no longer need expensive camera crews with big budgets. With your smart phone or any cheap camera, you can create your own video and upload them on Youtube in seconds.

There are three aspects to using video in your Social Media mix:

1. Programming and production of the video
2. Uploading and optimisation of the video
3. Publishing the video

Programming and production

Businesses can use video for a variety of topics; sponsored videos; product reviews, educational videos; live streaming; user-generated videos; how-to videos. Whether it is serious or fun there is a place for everybody and the more innovative your video will be, the more likely people will watch it and share it on Social Media.

So that brings the question, what is a good video? When will a video get a million hits? There are some basic rules that will help in achieving this.

The more ingredients a video has from the following list the more likely it will go viral:

- Controversial video
- Shocking video
- Educational video
- Funny video
- Informative video

People love funny videos. If you bring fun into your video, even if it is a business video, you are guaranteed to viral success. That's why children and pets work very well on video. Why do you think so many insurance companies use pets to make their brand come to live? Because insurance is a boring product and by introducing pets you can bring emotion and fun into your brand.

Another thing you have to ask yourself is what you want to achieve you are your business video. You can use it to introduce your company, your product or your service. Or you can use videos for product overviews, client success stories, finished projects etc.

Blendtec is a classic example. They sell industrial grade blenders used by companies like Starbucks and Caffe Nero. They made a video channel on Youtube and called it Will It Blend? They showcase the power of their blender by blending all kind of gadgets or items suggested by the public. Their hit videos include blending the iPhone and the iPad. They became an Internet legend overnight.

The nice thing about video nowadays is that it is completely do-it-yourself. It is very scalable. You can start very small, with a low budget. All you need is a video camera. You need to record your audio or you can do a video webcast, which is archiveable. You can do a live video webcast, you can do video collaboration or you can just make videos of slideshows.

The easiest way to make a simple video is via your smart phone. Every smart phone has a high-resolution camera and you can even download apps where you can do the video editing on your smart phone. A step up is the flip camera. It is a high-quality video camera with an integrated USB stick. You can upload the video directly on your laptop or desktop, and then upload it on Youtube. They are very simple, cheap and easy to use cameras. It fits in your pocket and works well for "quick-and-dirty" video recording. Most current SLRs, have high-quality video recording capabilities as well. Always look for the Full HD 1080p symbol on the video camera.

When you do a lot of interviews, get a semi-professional camera with "sound-in" because the quality of the sound is very important. When you do interviews, you really want to have a microphone on the collar of the person that you are interviewing so you have the best quality sound.

Always use a tripod in making your videos. Light is also very important. There's no better light than daylight, but if you haven't got daylight, make sure you have key light, fill light and a backlight if possible. Think about light very carefully. Remember when you think you have enough light, it might still be too dark.

Once you captured your video, you need to edit it. Microsoft comes standard with Movie Maker. Apple comes standard with iMovie. They both give you basic video editing functionality. If you want to be more advanced, there are tools like Apple Final Cut Pro or Adobe Premiere Pro. There are also editing facilities in Youtube. When you edit your video make sure you get a title in your video; you add background music; you use transitions; and you finish with a call to action, your website address and contact details. Also, make sure that the background music is legal.

You don't have to make a live video. You can also make a video of your photos as a slide show. Software companies who want to do a demo of their software can use screen-recording software to record the screen and capture mouse movements. This is great for software training and demos.

It is very important to plan your video. Why are you making your video? Who is your target market? What are the two key things you want people to remember when they watched your video? What problem do you solve with your video? How do you solve it? What makes you different? Think about those questions. A powerful tool you can use for this is a storyboard. Create a storyboard with the key messages, the key frames, the key scenes and transitions. This will be very helpful when you do your video shoot.

Uploading and Optimisation

The second step in the video process is publishing your video on Youtube and optimising it for playback and search. There are different ways of uploading your video on Youtube. If you make your video on your iPhone, you can share the video on Youtube via the sharing button in your camera roll. All you need is a google email account. You can also upload your video from your hard disk. You can record it from your webcam or you can make a video slideshow from your photos.

Once your video is uploaded on Youtube, there are various tools in Youtube to optimise your video to make sure that Google finds your video. We call this optimizing the metadata of your video. This includes:

- The title of your video
- The description
- The keywords
- The thumbnail of your video
- Annotations in your video
- Transcription of your video

It is very important that you have a very powerful title. People make a decision to watch a video based on the title of the video. If your title is weak, then that will not help towards generating more views for your video.

The description needs to be powerful as well and it needs to include your keywords. Always start your description with your website, your http website address because that gives you a link to your own website at your video page. There is nowhere else on your video page where you can link to a site outside Youtube. You can't link to a website in your video so you have to do that in your description. Think about your tags and think about all the other settings of your metadata.

There is also the optimisation of the thumbnails. What Youtube does is it will look at what frames are being used longest and it will pick those frames as your thumbnail, and then you can select which thumbnail you want for that. Youtube now also lets you upload your own thumbnail.

Youtube also has some basic editing options. You can trim your video, you can stabilize your video if it is shaky and there are different effects that you can do on your video.

When you watch videos on Youtube you often see little boxes popping up with messages or links to other videos. These are annotations. They can't link to a website, but they do link to other videos. What you see is that companies direct people to their latest video by showing an annotation at the beginning of the video saying "To see our latest video, click here." That's a good example of how an annotation can be used. It can also be used to add notes, a title or a spotlight. It is a very powerful feature in Youtube that you can control, edit and manage yourself.

Youtube also has some features to present your videos in a more organised and professional way. The most important feature is the Youtube Channel Page. When you create your Youtube Channel, you create your own branded social website on Youtube. It is like your Facebook Page except this is fully video-driven. You can have your Profile and your company branding in the banner. You can also have links to all your other Social Media sites. You want people to follow your Youtube Channel Page. As soon as you put up a new video, they get a notification. You create your own community around your videos.

The second feature is Playlists. You can create Playlists for different products, for different markets, for different topics. It is like a directory structure on your Channel Page. This is very powerful. Create your Youtube Channel with powerful branding and good playlists where people get access to your world of videos. You can subscribe to other Channels as well and they can feature on your Page. So all in all, Youtube becomes your full video-based Social Media channel. The more videos you publish, the more benefits you will get from setting up a Youtube Channel to promote your business.

A few more tips on Youtube:

- Make sure that you are active on your Youtube channel and that you regularly add new videos. You can participate by commenting, voting, subscribing, making playlists and publishing new videos. Make your Youtube Channel come to life.

- The first fifteen seconds of your video is key to capturing the viewer's attention. This is a great opportunity to add a subtle brand message to maintain engagement. Check your video analytics to see how long people stay on your video page. This can help you with programming your next video.

- Interact with other Youtube users because then they will promote your videos. Start building your network of Youtube users and engage with them to build relationships.

- Have a call to action in your videos. What do you want people to do after they've seen your video? Use annotations to create calls to action.

- Tag and label everything. Do this for every video that you post: give it labels; give it tags; give it a category; give it a powerful title. It is very important that you are consistent and that you use your keywords to make yourself searchable.

- Use annotations. You can give background information. You can use annotations to give people a menu of options to access your videos, and link to related Youtube videos, Channels or search results from within a video.

- Pay attention to detail, particularly on the thumbnails. The better your thumbnails, the more likely people will watch your video.

Publishing the video

This will be discussed in the Reach out Chapter.

Blogging

The best way to get started in Social Media is to start blogging. It is the easiest way to start creating your own social media content. Blog stands for Web Log. An online diary. It is been around for years and particular in the early years, people blogged for personal use, as their personal diary. When people travelled, they kept an online blog so people could follow their travel experiences. Nowadays, businesses have really picked up on blogs as a new way of engaging with their customers. They see it as a great way to share news and interesting information.

The power of blogging is that it is easy to start and easy to maintain. It is simple to create a blog post. Google loves blogs because a blog is fresh content. Google now rewards web sites that have regular, fresh and diverse content. Reward in this case means a higher position in the organic search results. The better your content, the more diverse your content, the better you feature your content on your site or your homepage, the more Google likes that. Anyone can start a blog. You go to www.wordpress.com or www.blogger.com, sign up, pick a template, press publish and your blog is up and running.

Search engines love blogs for the following reasons:

• They are very easily found because it is fresh content. The more entries you post, the more people will follow you and the more people will find you.

• Blogs have many Social Media features built in. It is hyperlinked. You put links to photos, videos or websites in your blog post. You have links on your blog page. You link to other bloggers. Bloggers love to link to each other. It is a global network of posts and that makes it so viral.

• Information can spread very quickly through blogs. More quickly than just having a static press release on your website. People love to share blogs and that makes them so viral.

• It is simple to subscribe to a blog. People can subscribe via email or RSS so they will get automatic updates of new blog posts.

• You can get the RSS feed of a blog on your own online listening station or your website. It is very linkable. Blogs link to each other. They love to link to each other and that's where you can go from one area to another area.

Internal Blogs

Blogging can be done very effectively within the organisation. Many people in IBM have their own blog which they use to share best practices and ideas with colleagues within the organisation. You can start a blog to replace your CEO's internal monthly newsletter. Internal Social Media can be used very effectively to test out how it works before you start using it externally.

External blogs

External blogs are an informal way to publish company news. It is a great way to ask customers for feedback, for their participation or ideas. It is a place to respond to public criticism or to comments. It is a way to interact with customers and clients on a more personal level. It is personal. It is not the company talking. You talk in name of the company. It is engaging, exciting, informal and conversational.

Blogging has been around for a long time and it has developed into a very powerful new communication tool for businesses. There are over 300 million blogs around the world at the moment, and millions and millions of blog posts are being posted everyday. The blog-reading community becomes bigger and bigger.

Bloggers are the new influencers. They are the new journalists. Many companies launch their products through bloggers instead of journalists. PR agencies have to reinvent themselves. Changing from being the "middle man" to the media, to being a value added content provider. Price-comparison websites need to reinvent themselves because people go to bloggers to read a review of the product that they want to buy before they go to price-comparison websites. Blogging has become a mainstream communication vehicle.

How to start your blog

There are various ways to get started with blogging. You have web-based blogging platforms and you can download the blogging platform on your own web server. The easiest way to get started is with a web-based blogging platform. It is simple to use, it is free or inexpensive, and they have lots of templates to choose from. The two leading ones are WordPress and Blogger. Blogger is owned by Google. Each blogging platform has its own set of features and characteristics, its own way of working and it depends on the user where he or she feels most comfortable in using it.

Wordpress.com

Wordpress is the world's leading blogging platform. Millions of blogs have been created with WordPress. Many people not only use Wordpress for their blog, but they have actually built their entire web site on wordpress.

Wordpress.com uses highly-customizable templates. It is easy to use and that's where wordpress really differentiates with other blogging platforms. It is a very user-friendly interface to create your blog, to maintain it and to add new blog posts. You can set up static pages so it looks like a traditional website.

With most hosted blogging platforms you can use a free version, but then your URL is (your name).bloggingplatform.com. If you pay a monthly fee, then you can link it to your own domain. So then it would be www.(your name).com. So it is basic functionality for free. You get more functionality, more templates for a monthly premium.

Wordpress.org

You can also download Wordpress on your own web server and host the site yourself. This is done through wordpress.org. You download the blogging software on your own hosting server, develop your wordpress blog and link the finished site to your domain name. Other downloadable blogging platforms are Movabletype or b2evolution.net.

How to integrate your blog with your web site?

An important thing to consider is how you are going to integrate your blog with your existing website. If your company website is developed on WordPress, you can just activate the blogging functionality and start blogging. Make sure you have a button on the homepage that links to the blog.

If your existing website doesn't have the functionality to add a blog, you can go to WordPress and create your own blog. Put the blog in the same look and feel as your website. Add a blog button on your existing website and link that button to your new WordPress blog. From an analytics point-of-view, it is not the ideal situation. But the customer won't notice. Make sure you open your blog as a new page or a new window so you don't lose the people from your website.

The components of a blog

A blog should have a standard set of modules. They are important to increase the virality of your blog.

Blog Avatar: Your blog avatar is your profile photo and your name. When multiple people blog on the same blog, the avatar can be a blog logo. Under that you then have small thumbnail photos plus names of the contributing bloggers.

About: Under your avatar, you have your "About". Who are you? What are you doing? What is this blog all about? It could be a different page, but in most blogs, it is under the avatar.

Tag Cloud: Under your about, you have a tag cloud. The tag cloud shows in one highlight what this person is blogging about. The bigger the words in the tag cloud, the more often that tag has been used. It gives a good summary of what this blog is all about. It is also an easy way to access previous blog posts. If you click one of the tags, you see a listing of all the blog posts with that tag. Some blogging platforms don't facilitate tag clouds. In this case, you can show the categories of the posts.

Recent posts/Popular posts: The recent posts section gives you a list of the latest blog posts. You can also show the most popular posts. These are the posts with the most comments. Again, it is about accessing older blog posts.

Blog roll: At the bottom you have your blog roll. Your blog roll is your top five to ten bloggers that you want to share with your followers.

Contact us: Create a contact section as well. That could be a different page or that could be on your blog page.

Social buttons: Make sure you have all your social media buttons on your blog's home page. Also add the relevant social sharing buttons to your blog posts. So people can share your blog posts on Facebook, on LinkedIn, on Twitter, on Google+, etc.

What to blog about?

The design of your blog is important, but the content is what really matters. Content is king. That's the main reason why people want to subscribe to your blog. You can have different types of posts:

1. Instructional posts tell people how to do something: how to use a product; how to use a service; how to use your software. It can be good for establishing yourself as an expert or building up a body of knowledge that you can refer to in the future. Most of the things I present in my workshops, I blog about as well. That is a knowledge base that I refer to during my

workshops.

2. Review posts to review a product or a service. People love to read about reviews and it can set you apart as a blogger. You can become an influential authority in your particular area. Bloggers about hotels, music, restaurants or cities, are leading influencers when it comes to promoting the product or service.

3. Lists are very popular in blogging. They can be lists of anything – your products, services, tips. They have titles like: "The 10 Ways to…", "The 7 Best Examples of…", "5 Things You Might Have Missed…" or "My Top 3 Tips to Do (This)…" It is good for search engine traffic and people love to search for top lists to find good content.

Blogging Calendar

Many people in my classes ask me how often they should do a blog update. You need to set yourself a target that you blog at least once a week. In your company you don't have to be the only person that blogs. If you assign two or three people, somebody in sales, management or customer service, and ask them to give input for a blog post once a month. Then you add these blog posts to your blogging calendar. So instead of you having to create a blog post every week, you ask your colleagues to produce one blog post each month. You put together a forward-looking calendar of blog posts based upon how often you want to post and then you can add regular posts like posting about an event, a wrap-up at the end of the month, the customer experience or a market trend. A blog calendar can really help in planning your blogs.

A blog doesn't have to be long. As long as it is good, valuable content. Better a short blog with one or two paragraphs with very good content than a blog with very poor content and six pages.

Also remember to add links and photos in your blogs. Make it visually appealing, and link it to other blogs and other sites.

Copyright images should not be used without permission. If you see a powerful image on the web and it is not copyright you can use it as long as you mention the source. There are lots of places where you can find free photos on the web.

Basic communication rules apply to blogging: Be professional. Don't be offensive. Blog regularly. Focus on a single topic. Ask before you start writing a blog what is the main thing you want people to remember? Think about the blog title. Use keywords in your title. Make it easily readable with clear fonts and make sure there are no typos. But in the end, it comes down to:

- Be interesting
- Have an opinion.
- Offer something unique related to your niche.
- Blog regularly.
- Be an authority.
- Find a voice.
- Be transparent.
- Be honest.
- Reveal your sources and partnerships.
- Tag your blog post.
- Use categories.
- Use keywords.

Use direct, simple language. Don't use overcomplicated words. Incorporate your keywords in your blog post, but don't overuse them. Use active verbs. For example, "The pilot flew the plane," rather than, "The plane was flown by the pilot." It is shorter, crisper and more dynamic. Use "you" and "we" to establish the relationship and draw the reader in. Use examples. Be conversational. Be yourself.

When you are ready for a company blog, you need to plan this carefully. They are inexpensive to start and maintain, but they can take time. So consider how your company will manage the blogs. The questions you need to ask yourself: Who will be posting? How often will we post? Are certain topics off-limits? How will you handle comments?

Comments

It is very important that you open your blog for comments so people can communicate and engage with you. It allows you to get into conversations with your readers. If you get lots of comments, you need to be able to deal with that. Always try to respond to comments. Both the positive and the negative. Try to understand the issue if it is a negative comment, try not to argue. If it runs out of control, then take it offline. If a comment is obscene, just remove it. Some blogs are being targeted by spammers so you need to have moderation in place. Wordpress will do this for you. You can set Wordpress to filter comments for SPAM and put them in a "waiting for approval" mode.

Blogosphere

Become active in the blogosphere, the community of bloggers that are relevant for your business. Bloggers can influence what people say about your company even if you choose not to blog. People can write about you in blogs. So participate and listen to what people are saying. Keep track of what is being said. Respond to posts and comments on other blogs. Unhappy customers often do not contact the company. They blog about it. So use blogs to pinpoint and solve problems quickly, and manage the comments.

REACHING OUT

"Never reach out your hand unless you are willing to extend an arm."

Pope Paul VI

The fourth step in setting yourself up for Social Media success is the Reaching Out phase. The essence of this phase is that if you are on Facebook, on LinkedIn or on Twitter, but you are not telling anybody, you won't grow your follower base and people won't engage with you. If you are not sharing any of your content, people won't find you and it won't help in developing your online reputation. That is why reaching out is such an important phase.

Reaching out is about creating the touch points where people can experience your content, experience the title of your blog post, experience the thumbnail of your video or experience an article about you. They get excited. They want to know more about you so they will read your blog and they might even register for blog updates. If they get really excited, they go to your website where they will buy your product or service.

You create as many touch points as possible when you reach out. You do that with your existing content, your blog post, your tweet or your video. But you also repurpose your content. You can convert your blog post into a PDF and share that on an article-sharing site. Or you change your blog post into a set of slides, and you share that on SlideShare. It is about driving traffic back to your website. This will help in building your online reputation and improving your search engine rankings.

Registering your blog

The first thing you do is to spread your blog. There are a few things you need to do before you launch your blog and publish your blog posts. It is important that you tell Google, Bing and Yahoo that you have a blog. You have to sign up for Google Webmasters, Yahoo Webmasters and Bing Webmasters and register your website or your blog with them. So at least the main search engines are aware of your existence.

There are also quite a few blog directories on the web. You have to register on these too. As mentioned earlier, Technorati is one of the leading blog directories. Sign up with Technorati and claim your blog. When you register your blog, Technorati will give you a code. You need to add that code somewhere on your blog. When technorati verifies that you are the owner of the blog it will search for the code on your blog. And when they find it they will confirm the blog is yours.

There are other sites like BlogCatalog. They will ask you in return to add a BlogCatalog button on your website as part of the confirmation process.

You should also bookmark your site on key bookmarking sites so at least your blog is known on those websites. Then there are lots of other places where you can go to if you want to spread your blog any further. When you search on the web for "where to register my blog" you get many links to sites where you can register. And obviously, the more places you register your blog at, the more exposure your blog will get.

Spreading your (blog) updates

The next step is to spread your (blog) updates to all your relevant social networks. One of the leading tools for this is HootSuite. HootSuite will help you broadcast to all your social networks through a simple dashboard interface. On your dashboard you can have a separate stream for each of your social networks. And it will assist you in creating, scheduling and sending your updates. You can select which of your social networks an update should go to. So basically, you let HootSuite do the broadcasting for you. You don't have to go in each social network to spread your messages. You let HootSuite do that. It allows you to repurpose your content with different messages across different networks. You can also schedule and filter messages that you send out. There is a collaboration feature so your boss will get an e-mail to approve a message before it is going out. You can also define search channels so it can work really well for lead generation. There are many other features on HootSuite like analytics, an inbuilt URL shortener and saving messages as drafts. You can also get the pro version which will give you additional features.

Once you've spread it, it will feature differently across different networks. But the essence is the same. People will see your content. They can comment on it, like it, share it and click on the link to take them to the source of the content. That is why the title and the thumbnail in your post are so important. People will often make a decision to click on a link, based on the title or the thumbnail.

Repurposing your content

To boost your content even further, it is important to repurpose your content. This means that you convert your existing piece of content into another format and share it on sites relevant to that format. Transform your blog post into a set of slides and upload on SlideShare. SlideShare gives me a lot of traffic to my website and it is a great reference for people. A lot of people search on slideshare for good content. By putting your blog post on Slideshare, you will develop your online reputation. You can also record the set of slides and turn it into a video that you can upload on video sharing sites like Youtube or Vimeo. This will give you additional traffic. Of course in the presentation and in the video, the last slide should be the link to your website where people can read the full blog post. And mention this in the description as well.

Notifications

Notifications are very important in the reaching out phase. People can subscribe to your blog which means that every time you do a blog update, they will receive a notification email. There is a genuine place for e-mail in Social Media. Email is changing from a messaging platform to a notification platform. Newsletters are no longer lengthy e-mails with pages of information, but they are notifications which link to different places on the web or different places on your Social Media sites where people can find more information.

When you have new content like a blog post or an eBook, you write a short e-mail with a summary of the content and with a strong title. At the bottom you say "Click here to read more". This will take the reader to the source. This could be your blog post or the page where people can download the e-book. You can use tools like MailChimp or Constant Contact to manage these emails for you. The power of these e-mail systems is that you can see who opened the e-mail and what links they clicked on.

Always make sure you ask people permission to email them and you give them an option to unsubscribe. You need to build a clean database. "Permission" is a flexible word, but you can ask permission when you meet them at events or in a telemarketing campaign, or in a contact form on your web site. When I run my training sessions, I ask people for permission to add them to my mailing list. Make sure that you build a targeted mailing list.

Spreading your videos

As mentioned in the Youtube chapter, there are three aspects to using video in your Social Media: The production of the video, the publishing and optimisation of the video on Youtube and the promotion of your video. You promote your videos by spreading them across your social networks and them to your own website. One of the main benefits of Youtube is that it has a number of features that can help you to spread your video outside Youtube. The basic rule here is to embed your Youtube videos in your own website. To do this you click the share button under the video you want to share in Youtube. You select Embed, you define the size of the video, you get an embed code and you copy that code in your website. When people play it from your website, it will still count as a view in Youtube. This is very important. Google rewards you in search rankings when you have a video on your homepage.

Here are some other tips to promote your videos:

- Add links from your website to your Youtube channel
- Announce those links on your Twitter and Facebook
- Get people to link to your Youtube channel
- Tell your customers that you are on Youtube
- Promote your videos on Facebook and Twitter
- Use Advertising in Youtube and Google to promote your videos
- Promote your videos on other video platforms like Vimeo, Flick TV, Vimeo, Viddler or TubeMogul

Also make sure you link your Youtube channel with your Facebook Page. In your Facebook Page, get an App with your videos. Integrating Youtube with your blog is important as well. If you have a WordPress blog you can use Youtube widgets to add video to your blog.

Content Syndication

There is another aspect of Reaching out and that is sharing other people's content. This type of content sharing is called content syndication. You scan the web on good content and when you see an interesting article, you share that article with your followers on your own social networks. This can have different formats. The simplest way of sharing interesting content is by using the sharing buttons that you now see on many articles online. You can share it on Facebook, you can Tweet it, you can share it on LinkedIn or you can share it on Google+. When you see a +1 button that means that you share it on Google+. By clicking one of these sharing buttons you will get a little popup window with the highlight and the visual of the article. You can add your own remarks to the post and share it on your social networks. That's the most effective way of sharing. I do a lot of this type of sharing when I commute. On my iPhone I have an app called FlipShare. It gives me news and Social Media content that I can flip through. When I see an interesting article, I share it on my Facebook, my LinkedIn or I tweet about it.

Don't overdo it. Social Media is about driving people to your web site. And you don't want to drive them too much to other people's web sites. Use this type of sharing wisely. Done correctly, it will help you in developing your profile to become an expert in your field.

You can do this content syndication in batches as well. You can use Bufferapp.com to schedule the content you find. It allows you to fill up your Buffer at any time in the day and Buffer automatically posts them for you through the day, at the times that you specify. Simply keep that Buffer topped up to have a consistent social media presence all day round, all week long.

You don't have to scan the web yourself for interesting content. Paper.li is a content curation service that enables you to monitor content and topics across the web, turning content into beautiful online newspapers and newsletters. Once you tell Paper.li what type of content you would like to monitor, they scout the web and present the content you want, when you want, automatically. There are also tools like Storify.com where you can gather news around topics and put them in story boards that you can share.

TRACK

"You cannot improve what you cannot measure"
Lord Kelvin

The last section of FLIRT is Track: The measurement or analysis of your Social Media activities so you can learn from it, you can improve on it and you can adjust your strategy based on the findings of your analysis.

It is a vital part of your Social Media. It is a vital part of any strategy that you set up. Do we achieve our objectives? It all starts with the statement from Lord Kelvin, "You cannot improve what you cannot measure." That's the reason why we measure.

Media and measurement have changed considerably since arrival of digital communications in the late-90s and the early-2000s. The traditional media and measurement that we know from the 90s was measuring effectiveness of

TV advertising, print advertising, radio advertising, word of mouth or direct mail. They were fairly simple to measure. It was difficult to put a value on them, but you could measure your reach and your audience. You could reach out to the customer through telephone surveys or focus groups. You could test and find out about how customers were feeling. After the sale, you could get data in relation to the warranty, the credit card and the payment info.

The arrival of online advertising and search put a new dimension to the media and measurement in the early-2000s. With Google AdWords and banner advertising, different ways of measurement became available. You wanted to know: How many clicks do I get on a certain page? How many page views do I get for the different pages on my website? How long do people stay on my website? How many people registered for my newsletter? How many opt-ins did we get to some of the calls to action that we had on the website? It became a lot more complex, but also a lot more specific on the results that you got out of your online campaigns. There is also the effectiveness of the search. What position do you get on the search engine rankings? What is the growth of your position on the search engine rankings? What keywords do work? What keywords do not work? This led to a whole new online discipline. The discipline of SEO, Search Engine Optimisation. SEO agencies popped up everywhere and it was the cool thing to do in the mid 2000s. Companies spent thousands and thousands of pounds to make sure their SEO was top notch.

Then towards the end of the 1st decennium of the 2000s, Social Media brought a whole new range of measurement metrics. How many likes did we get? How many comments did we get? How many reviews did we get on our product? How many fans do we have? How many

Posts do we do? How many product reviews? How many Retweets? How many people bookmarked our Page? How many Views did we get on our Videos? How many people shared our posts? From a marketing perspective, you could be a lot more specific in how you measure the effectiveness of your marketing and Social Media campaigns.

3 types of metrics

There are 3 types of marketing metrics for your Social Media. You can measure your activities, the consumer response and the business outcomes.

Measuring your activities: Activities are things like how many Videos did we Post? How many Tweets did we send? How many online media did we serve? How many blog posts did we do? How many links did we put in blog posts? How many Comments did we do ourselves on other blog posts? It is these types of activities that you can plan ahead and just measure yourself on the effectiveness of your outreach.

Measuring consumer response: How do customers respond to our Social Media outreach? Are there changes in perception like intent to purchase or customer satisfaction? How many Likes did we get? How many new fans did we get? How many downloads? How many clicks on our website? How many people filled in the response form on the web site? For how many of our customers or prospects do we have their shopping preferences?

Measuring business outcomes: This type of measurement is important for management. How much money did we make? How much money did we save? What is the return on investment? Other business outcomes can be found in market share, staff retention, or customer sale cycle time.

Measuring your online reputation

At the highest level, measuring social media is like measuring brand value. Brand value is very closely related to reputation. Nowadays in the online world, we're talking about your online reputation. You want to come up with a score for your online reputation. What do people say when they talk about you? What impression do people have of your online behavior? What are they saying about your product, your brand, your reputation and your competition?

Managing and understanding your online reputation can really help you in developing your word of mouth, in increasing customer loyalty, in generating new ideas to bring into the organisation, in increasing your product and brand awareness; to improve the effectiveness of your public relations; to reduce customer acquisition cost; to reduce customer support cost; to reduce market research cost; and to reduce product development cost.

By understanding your online reputation, you can also identify the influencers. By analysing what is being said, you can understand it and you can find out who is saying what. Who are the key influencers? How can you connect with those influencers? You can develop a direct communication with those influencers. By understanding and analysing your online reputation, you can also identify the topics that people are talking about. You can respond to these topics or use them as input for new content you want to share.

Yesterday was about brand value. Today is about online reputation. It doesn't mean that brands and brand value is gone. But there is a new component to this and that is your online reputation. This online reputation works almost the opposite of how traditional brands works.

How would you define your online reputation? It is influenced by all the visible content available online about your company, your products and services, your employees, your partners, and your affiliates, clients and suppliers.

Earned media is more trusted by consumers, candidates and partners by far. This means it is important to monitor what is being said on the web and to work on these touch points. Make sure that you listen and that you participate in the places where those stakeholders have conversations with you.

Like your brand value is built over a long time, your online reputation has to be build long-term. It is not a short term campaign. It takes time, effort and dedication. But it is built almost completely opposite the way traditional brands have been built. And you can ruin your online reputation in a split second.

Measuring your online reputation

So how do you analyse your online reputation? How do you measure it? Really important is that you understand the four factors that contribute to a brand's online reputation.

Volume. How much content is there on the web about you, about your brand, about your company? When I search for your company, how much volume comes up and how much of that volume relates to you?

Relevance. How consistent is the content that comes up with you and who you say you are? How consistent is it with how you want to be seen on the web?

Diversity. How diverse is your web content? If it is just text, your online reputation will score lower than if it is a combination of photo, video, sound and text.

Purity. How much of the content is related to you, to your business. The name of your company plays an important role in this. If you have a unique name, then you will score higher on the purity than if you don't have a unique name. When you have a unique name, you will have less competition online to compete for the top search rankings.

By doing searches on Google and then analyzing it on volume, relevance, diversity and purity, you can come up with a very accurate score of your online reputation.

4 types of brands

One thing you need to take into consideration when you analyse your online reputation is the personality of your brand. It is a fact that some brands are more social. In other words, some brands are being talked about more than other brands. You need to know for yourself where you are as a brand to understand the type of Social Media, the type of content and the type of outreach you need to do.

There is a basic brand, a functional brand, an exciting brand and a vital brand. The level of Social Media outreach and the level of engagement will be different per brand.

Basic brands: There will be very little on the web about you because there's no reason for people to talk about you. So there are few conversations. There's no need for people to be positive or negative about you so you will probably have a very basic presence on Social Media and very limited comments. So what you do as a basic brand is to try to make yourself exciting or set yourself apart from your competition by being funny or by making yourself somehow useful. A really good example of this is Blendtec. I talked about them in an earlier chapter.

Functional brands. These brands will have more conversations around them. There is more tendency that people will like or dislike them. So they will have a higher presence on Social Media. They need to listen to and participate in conversations. People want to be able to ask questions and get answers. They want to understand the product and people will search for product reviews. It is important when you are a functional brand, to engage in Social Media to help people find answers they have on the product, thereby improving customer satisfaction, getting better marketing understanding, improving your customer service and decreasing your customer service costs.

There are functional brands like Best Buy. They came up with Twelp Force where they offer people answers to basic questions they could ask on Twitter. They succeeded in that by uniting all of their specialists of all their products in one place, offering functional advice to their customers. That was a very genuine reason. As a functional brand, that's the best way to drive your Social Media.

Exciting brands. When you are an exciting brand, there is no problem in getting people to talk about you. They will be positive or negative so you need to have a high presence on Social Media. There will be lots of comments on everything that you share online. Coca Cola doesn't have a problem in getting millions of Facebook Friends because people love to talk about the brand and they love to collect everything that Coca Cola makes available on their

Facebook Page. But the problem is that not many brands are exciting. You need to try to make your brand more exciting. That is all about getting really good content available for your followers.

Vital brands. As a vital brand, you will have lots of conversations and hopefully good sentiments. You will be present on Social Media and lots of people will have comments on whatever you do. These are brands that affect people in a very direct manner like health or the environment. For these brands, it is vital that you listen very carefully to what people are saying. These are brands that are at risk for crisis situations. They need to listen carefully to make sure that they anticipate a crisis and know how to deal with it.

Don't box yourself into just one brand type, but get an understanding where you are and try to move up a bit to make yourself more exciting as a brand. Start small, but think big. Monitor your online conversations and then respond, accept that you might not know what your best strategy is yet. But you have to test.

What to measure on your social networks?

For simple measurement of your Social Media, you have to go to the different social networks. They all have their own Social Media analytics. The quality of the analytics varies substantially per platform. Facebook is very advanced on the analytics. LinkedIn is less advanced on analytics. Expect those Social Media networks that are lagging behind to catch up soon.

Also remember that your Social Media will only work if you have consistency between your Social Media sites from a content and a campaign point of view. So your measurement must go across your social networks.

There are three types of data that you can get from the different Social Media platforms.

Traffic Analysis: This is the simple type of data. How many Page views? How many unique visitors? How many bounce rates? How many popular pages? How many returning visitors? How many search terms?

When it comes to traffic measurement, the best measurement tool is Google Analytics. You need to register your website in Google Analytics. Google will give you a unique code that you can add to each page that you want to be measured. From the moment you put that code into your website, Google will then be able to measure the performance of your website. Another site where you can get basic site information is Alexa.

Traffic can also be measured for Twitter. How many Tweets did you send? How many Retweets did you do and how many Retweets did you get? How many Followers did you get and how many people are you Following? What is the total audience reach? What are the key messages? How many links did you add to your Tweets?

Two Twitter tools are worth looking at. Tweetstats.com will give you an overview of your Twitter activity. How many Tweets per day? What times are your Tweets being sent out? What is your Tweet density? What are your reply statistics? It gives you some really good data about your Twitter behavior. If you want to measure the effectiveness of your Tweets, a really good tool to use is TweetReach. This will give you data like: How many people did you reach? What is your exposure? What is your activity level?

Engagement Analysis: The second level of measurement is engagement analytics. How do my Followers engage with my content? How many Friends? How many Followers? How many Likes? How many Retweets? How many Comments? How many uploads? How many Referrals? How many people participated in your polls? etc.

Facebook Insights provides really good analytics around your pages and metrics around the content. You can assess the performance data of your Page. You can learn which content resonates with your audience and which content doesn't. Then you can optimise how you can publish to your audience so that people will tell their friends about this. Facebook has also very good advertising analytics. This will give you access to a Facebook Advertising Dashboard that will show you the increase in clicks, in actions on your website. You get a percentage on click-through rates and a good view of how much you spent on this.

LinkedIn does not come with rich measurement dashboards. But there are a few good bits of pieces of analytics in LinkedIn. Particularly the groups' analytics and the company page analytics. Before you join a group, always check the group analytics and particularly, the activity level. In the activity level, you can see how many discussions have been posted and how many comments have been made so you know what the interaction is. It is also important to check the demographics to see what type of seniority and what the locations are. If this is outside your target market or outside your seniority level, then it is not worth joining that group. Company analytics are quite powerful as well where you can see the number of Page views, the number of unique visitors, the Page clicks and you can see the Page visitor demographics.

Youtube has Google analytics grade quality of analysing your videos. Youtube Analytics is a robust tool that provides informative data and insight about your content, your audience and your programming. Use the analytics to come up with better videos that will create more views in the future.

Sentiment Analysis: Finally, you can measure the sentiment. Are people positive or are people negative about you? In order to do this you need to analyse text. You need to search in your comments for instance on keywords, trends, positives, negatives etc. Big global consumer brands rely heavily on this type of analytics and they invest large sums of money in getting the right software to do this sentiment analysis.

Your analytics dashboard

Going to each social network to do the analytics and then to bring it all together in one management summary can be a big task. It is a bit like your online listening. You don't want to go to every web site you want to listen to. You want to let them come to you through RSS feeds, in your online listening station. You can do the same with your analytics. There are tools like Social Oomph that will do all the analytics work for you. It will connect with all your social networks and pull the data from each site. They will then bring it into their own analytics reports that you can slice and dice in any format you like. By setting up your analytics dashboard you have immediate data available when you need it and you can summarise your analytics reports per social network individually or aggregated into one Social Media report.

MARC CAMPMAN

ABOUT THE AUTHOR

Marc Campman is a social media playmaker. He turns your social media content into stories and your stories into plays. He is a multi- award winning international marketing and social media specialist. Marc's experience spans over 30 years of marketing and sales in the technology, telecoms and gaming business in a wide variety of companies, from large global organisations to local startups. Over the years he has built up extensive expertise in every area of traditional and online marketing. With his experience in online marketing and Social Media, he can be considered a thought leader in Social Media and Content Marketing.

Social Media Marketing is all about creating your own plays. Plays to make connections, participate in conversations and generate ideas. Social Media Marketing is word of mouth on steroids. If you haven't got your plays ready, you will be left behind. Marc lectures and presents about today's best Social Media marketing plays and shares his experience with businesses, helping them to start conversations, create communities, advance ideas and seed discussions.

His experience in Social Media is in depth and diverse. Besides having sold and implemented enterprise Social Media solutions for companies like Unilever and Global Radio, he has first hand experience in launching big Social Media campaigns for brands like MNE (IPC Media) targeting bands and Random House targeting reading clubs.

Marc is a regular blogger on the topic of Social Media content (www.marccampman.com) and is an active user of most Social Media networks and tools. It is his firm belief that you can only teach about Social Media if you are an active social networker yourself.

Marc is co-founder of Love Social Media, a Social Media training company based in London. Love Social Media challenges the relationships that companies have with their customers. They offer social media training and services that are getting to the heart of customer conversations and relationships.

Additionally, Marc teaches at various other training institutions like the MiH Academy in Dubai, the Corporate Communications Centre at the Erasmus University in Rotterdam and the Career Development Center at the American Chamber of Commerce in Cairo.

People from a wide range of companies have attended his Social Media training classes and as a result he is being hired by many companies to run in-house marketing, sales and management workshops on Social Media and advise them on Social Media strategy and implementation. These include companies like Douwe Egberts, Etisalat, Hilton Hotels and Resorts, MAF Ventures, ABB limited, Real Asset Management, bss, Cornish Mutual, National School of Government, AED Practice and Absolute Strategy Research ltd.